Dignidad

ETHICS THROUGH HISPANIC EYES

Ismael García

ABINGDON PRESS
NASHVILLE

DIGNIDAD: ETHICS THROUGH HISPANIC EYES

This book is printed on acid-free, recycled paper.

Library of Congress Cataloging-in-Publication Data

García, Ismael, 1947–
    Dignidad: ethics through Hispanic eyes / Ismael García.
      p.   cm.
    Includes bibliographical references and index.
    ISBN 0-687-02134-0 (pbk.: alk. paper)
    1. Hispanic Americans—Religion.   2. Christian ethics—United
States.   3. Hispanic Americans—Social life and customs.   I. Title.
BR563.H57G37   1997
241'.089'68073—dc21

                                                         97-9143
                                                            CIP

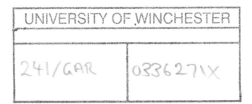
97 98 99 00 01 02 03 04 05 06—10 9 8 7 6 5 4 3 2 1

MANUFACTURED IN THE UNITED STATES OF AMERICA

To my parents, Ismael García Rios and Matilde Rios Cuevas, who taught me that dignity is expressed through the virtues of hard work, cultural pride, courage, and perseverance in the quest for justice, compassion, service, and care for the needy.

CONTENTS

PREFACE

It is frustrating to have to admit that one cannot give due honor and recognition to all those who made this text possible. Many are the ones to whom I am indebted in the preparation of the ideas presented here. Let me at least recognize and give due mention to those few without whose contributions and support this project would never have come to maturity. This text was commissioned by the members of the Mexican American Program and the Hispanic Instructors Group at Perkins School of Theology. I am extremely grateful to Roy Barton, who is in his last year of service as Director of this program, to Justo L. González for the many ways he has supported this project, and to the Hispanic Instructors who have been faithful custodians of my progress in writing this book.

I was the beneficiary of a number of the excellent events held at Perkins by the Mexican American Program. The one which will always stand out in my mind was the three-year theological symposia that examined the implications of the 1492 landing of Europeans on the continent we know today as America. Hispanic American and Latin American theologians, social scientists, historians, and pastors presented what will become one of the best collections on this topic. I have also had the pleasure of teaching with the Hispanic Instructors during the summer program at Perkins. In this context I had the opportunity to meet the candidates for ministry in The United Methodist Church that will serve Hispanic communities. All of us who are interested in Hispanic ministry and Hispanic theology also owe a deep debt of gratitude to the journal *Apuntes* which, for more than fifteen years, has provided an ecumenical and multidisciplinary medium for Hispanics to engage in creative and constructive ethical reflection.

During December 1994 at the Hispanic Instructors annual meeting, I was asked to present an outline of my work. I was encouraged and motivated by their support and by the critical comments the Hispanic Instructors made about my proposal. I made some revisions in light of the conversation we had that day, and incorporated some of the views and concerns expressed during that meeting. They were the ones who suggested that a book dealing with Hispanic ethics had to carry the title *Dignidad* which, in their view, is a significant part of the Hispanic moral point of view. Last December 1995, I presented the manuscript to the group. It was carefully and thoughtfully criticized by Justo L. González, Harold Recinos, Luis Pedraja, and the Reverend Mr. G. Chávez. The manuscript was once again revised in light of their quite helpful and insightful suggestions.

It is my hope that this text be a mixture of my insights as a Hispanic Christian ethicist and of the ethical insights of Hispanic Americans who struggle to be faithful to the gospel of Jesus Christ as they minister in this nation. I have tried to be as inclusive as possible, and as fair as possible when I consider the diverse ways Hispanics speak the language of ethics and make ethical choices. Not all Hispanics agree, nor need they agree, with some of the constructive proposals I make. My hope is, however, that all will continue to engage me in conversation. One of the things that makes Hispanic theological reflection unique, refreshing, and constructive is that we are less interested in "scoring points against each other" and more interested in contributing to each other's work so it might be of service to the church and the formation of ministers seeking to serve our community.

Thanks have to be given to Austin Presbyterian Theological Seminary, not only for providing a context that encourages serious academic work among its faculty and students, but whose generous sabbatical program allowed me to dedicate time to this project. My colleagues have influenced and improved my teaching and research in ways they are not aware of.

Special thanks go to Ann Rosewall García, my wife, who unselfishly gave of her time so that I might have the freedom to write, who in ways that manifest her loving nature gave me much-needed support and encouragement, and who read and corrected the manuscripts innumerable times, making my Spanish mind-set intelligible to English readers. But more important, Ann's critical comments have played a substantial role in shaping some of the ideas in this book. As a hospital chaplain who is frequently called to translate and attend to the fears and concerns of Spanish-speaking patients, she has also made me acutely aware of the many subtle ways Hispanics appeal to their theological and ethical beliefs to overcome the oppression and domination to which they are subjected. She is one of my sources about the lived life of those who do not have much power, social standing, or economic resources. I owe her thanks but most of all I promise her my love.

INTRODUCTION

From a Hispanic point of view, moral reasoning, the kind of reasoning that makes us feel intimately bound to it and that elicits from us a passionate response, is not the product of mere abstract thinking.[1] Moral rationality is intrinsically intertwined with at least three elements: (1) our communally induced feelings and shared understandings of what is right and good, of what is wrong and bad; (2) the habitual and traditional ways our communities organize their day-to-day practices and institutionalize their understanding of the good and right, bad and wrong; and finally, (3) traditional cultural practices and abiding religious convictions which, even if we cannot prove them true or false to the uninitiated, still enable us to confess in a clear and intelligible way that which constitutes the ultimate ground of our moral commitments. Feelings, traditions, cultural habits, and religious convictions are part of the act of thinking about moral behavior. Therefore, our perceptions of God, our differing social experiences and cultural manners influence and shape the ways we feel, practice, and think about the moral life. The purpose of this book is to clarify how these various elements become part of the Hispanic moral point of view.

Hispanics emphasize the social nature of morality. We acknowledge that we are born into communities with shared moral beliefs and practices that provide their members with a broad understanding of what is morally good and right. Every political community, through its main institutions (family, school, church, and a plurality of neighborhood and voluntary associations), attempts to socialize us, with varying degrees of success, into its vision of the good person and the just society. Within free societies it is not uncommon that different social groups within the community develop diverse and even conflictual moral points of view. Plurality in moral visions normally results from the moral conflict that emerges between a well-defined social group and the dominant social institutions they live in. Our *comunidad* will attempt to socialize and incorporate us into its particular moral vision. This is an intrinsic part of the process by which we develop the conscience of being members of a people with a unique identity. Hispanic ethics has its starting point in those shared moral insights and practices of our immediate communities and the affinities and tensions our community has with the larger political community we belong to. Our ethical reflection is nothing other than our reflections, on a somewhat higher level of abstraction, on our day-to-day moral practices as we seek to go forward with a shared life worthy of the name "good."

The moral understanding and ways of Hispanics are closely tied to our being members of well-defined ethnic groups. Group life, especially when it is defined by ethnicity and race, is a basic reality that shapes our conception of self and morality. Unlike voluntary associations, group life entails having a common history, generally sharing a way of life, language, religion, and social identity.[2] Our morality is influenced as much by the positive and negative elements of our Hispanic culture as by the positive and negative experiences we must respond to within Anglo Saxon culture.

Our morality is also social in the more fundamental sense that it acknowledges that the inclination to be concerned for others, the disposition of having *other regard*, is an essential element of any authentic morality. We received this insight from our Christian religious heritage, which defines morality as being centered in the fact that we are relational beings. At the heart of Christian ethics is the confession that we gain life by surrendering it for the well-being of others. Morally speaking, life is for the sake of giving and receiving care in ways that are loving and just, and in ever-widening circles of inclusiveness. We become fully human through our relationships with "others." By recognizing and caring for "others," we are able to realize or fulfill the goodness of our being and our life. If we were not capable of being other-directed, our life would be brutish, poor, and short. An exaggerated focus on self-fulfillment would be self-defeating for our becoming more and living in community with others. Human wholeness takes place not when we seek it in a deliberate way, but rather when we meet others and struggle for the satisfactions of our mutual needs. This leads Hispanics to give priority to care, responsibilities, and connectedness over separation, individual achievement, and individual rights. Interpersonal social relationships cement our sense of respect for others and adherence to moral standards. In creating more inclusive relationships, we comprehend the meaning and purpose of moral values. We define who we are, and unveil our dignity and worth, through the relationships of mutual aid we have with others. In chapter 1 we examine the way Hispanics express the disposition of "other regard" through the formulation of principles, the development of character traits, and the creation of structures of care and mutual recognition.

Hispanic moral conscience entails awareness of the interdependent nature of social reality and the corresponding responsibility for considering how our actions impinge on the lives of others. When we act, our actions will either contribute to or hinder the well-being of others, and as such they are inherently related not only to what it means to be human but also to the possibility of creating and sustaining community. This is why justice is such a central concern of the Hispanic point of view. In chapter 2, we examine the different ways Hispanics struggle for social justice and the value content of these different struggles.

Besides an emphasis on the social, a strong sense of personhood shapes the moral point of view of most Hispanics. This is particularly true among Hispanics who ground their moral point of view on religious convictions. We do not conceive of God primarily in philosophical categories; rather we use the language and imagery of personal relationships. We view God as a companion, a friend, a source of care, support, and hope. Our everyday language is full of God talk: "hay Dios," "Dios te bendiga," "que sea la voluntad de Dios," "Ave María." We express ourselves in ways that reveal our sense of the ever-presence of God in our lives. Chapter 3 lifts up the theological dimensions which are present in the Hispanic moral points of view, and in chapter 4 we argue for a vision of the church that lifts up the moral concerns of Hispanics.

From a Hispanic point of view moral agency entails more than mere conformity to dominant moral precepts, or mere imitation of those persons the dominant political community emulates as good and righteous. Authentic moral agency assumes that each person has the capacity to engage in careful examination and scrutiny of the principles and visions of the prevalent moral order, and the moral wisdom embedded in our traditions. It assumes that we can make an informed, voluntary, and intimate commitment to those values we come to recognize as worthy of our loyalty. In a sense we become moral agents through a process similar to our becoming religious beings. We can make our children go to church, study Scripture, bow their heads when we pray, and stand and act reverently when expected. But they will become religious when they accept, make a personal choice for, and commit themselves to respond faithfully to the call God and the community of faith extend to them. Both morality and faith are grounded on freedom, and both of these are authentic when they secure, for all members of society, the freedom and skills necessary to make informed personal commitments. These freedoms and skills are necessary for us to be able to meet the new moral challenges that result from the human capacity to re-create our natural and social environment.

The affirmation and redefinition of identity and dignity is at the heart of the Hispanic moral quest. Our capacity for moral agency, our capacity to create community, and our capacity to be authentic to the values of our culture feed our sense of human dignity. Throughout the text I will attempt to articulate what Hispanics mean by human dignity and its implication for the moral life.

Hispanics who live in the United States have not yet devoted much energy to the task of formulating an ethical theory.[3] However, as a unique sociocultural group, we do have a contribution to make regarding moral reflection and the moral character of our society today. It ought to come as no surprise that the language through which we articulate our moral visions and commitments is not only diverse, but at times gives expression to conflicting moral points of view. These divergences and conflicts are a mere reflection of the fact that as members of a pluralistic society we are continuously exposed, and cannot but be influenced, in varying degrees, by the different social groups, with their own unique cultural, religious, and moral ways of life, that aggressively compete for our loyalty.

Furthermore, Hispanic Americans are quite a heterogeneous social group. Different subgroups within the Hispanic comunidad represent and have their roots in different national backgrounds. We are racially, economically, religiously, and culturally quite diverse. And though we share a common language, even here one finds an infinite richness and nuance of expression that forcefully reveal the singularity and uniqueness of each Hispanic subgroup. If it is true that multicultural interpretations of morality are quite likely to lead to different interpretations of reciprocity, friendship, care, and moral respect, it is also true that the internal diversity of our community and our exposure to the diverse moral points of view and commitments found within the larger society, cannot but affect the way Hispanics understand the moral institution of life.

What is unreasonable is to expect that Hispanics would speak with one voice and present a homogeneous moral point of view or engage only in one form of moral reasoning. We are, and will probably remain, quite eclectic in our moral understandings and commitments. Our moral points of view and sensibilities are nourished from abundant wells of visions and theories that flow from our Iberian, African, and Western heritage. As we attempt to uplift the dominant motifs and various styles of reasoning expressed in our moral language, we must do our best not to succumb to the temptation of reducing the eclecticism and diversity intrinsic to the moral reasoning of Hispanics, to one style or type of moral reasoning.

CHAPTER 1

HISPANIC STYLES
OF MORAL REASONING

Introductory Comments

I t is simply not possible to formulate *the* ethical theory that dominates Hispanic moral thinking. Our present task is the more
modest one of unveiling the dominant motifs found in the moral
language by which Hispanic Americans express their moral views and
commitments. As we examine the different styles of moral reasoning
used by Hispanics, I will point to the strengths and weaknesses of each
style. I will then show that although there is not one dominant style,
there are common motifs that represent the centerpieces of Hispanic
moral reflection. These dominant motifs cut across diverse ethical
points of view and come closer to what could be called a Hispanic moral
point of view or ethics through Hispanic eyes.

The dominant motifs that inform the different ethical views of
Hispanics are, to a great extent, a response to the social condition lived
by our people. We appeal to the terms "oppression" and "domination"
to both describe and evaluate the social conditions in which our people
are forced to live. In using the terms oppression and domination, our
purpose is to point to a multilayered social condition that covers the
diverse social harms inflicted on us as a social group. It is important to
specify and describe each of these social harms in order to understand
better how different manifestations of oppression relate to one another
and how each one is unique. Different subgroups within the larger
Hispanic community are affected more by one or another form of
oppression and domination; to be freed from them, each form of
oppression must be dealt with on its own terms.[1] To be oppressed is to

be subjected to a social structure in which the power and freedom needed by one social group to forward its self-realization is controlled or possessed by another social group.

ECONOMIC OPPRESSION

Economically speaking, oppression takes place when the labor and productivity of one social group benefits another social group. The poverty experienced by Hispanics is neither accidental nor fortuitous; it is the outcome of our particular system of production and of the culture of discrimination under which we presently live. The structure of production determines the limits of the labor force: who will work and how long they will work. The culture of discrimination is influential in determining which social group is most likely to be left out. Put both of these factors together, and we have a better sense of why it is that many capable Hispanic men and women are undertrained and many more are underemployed. It also helps us understand why unemployment, which keeps Hispanics marginal to the social process of production and consumption, is disproportionately high among our people.[2]

Our community is poor because our participation within the labor force is limited to those activities that are seasonal, temporal, or poorly remunerated. We are locked into jobs that are menial, boring, and unfulfilling. Although they are socially necessary, useful, and contribute significantly to our nation's economy, we are poorly or unequally compensated for our labor. This is particularly true for women. Although they perform similar work and their productivity is relatively equal, they are paid significantly less for their work. When one considers that many of these women are also single parents, one can understand why working mothers and an inordinate percentage of Hispanic children are still below the poverty line.

Being poor entails much more than lacking material goods. It also entails being unable to satisfy the ideals of the good life widely propagated by our society. This condition feeds the sense of impotence, fatalism, and lack of worth that affects many Hispanics, particularly the young. In a consumer society like the one in which we live, if one cannot buy and be an active "market agent," one does not really count and is not noticed. In our society, lacking money threatens our publicly perceived sense of dignity and worth, and our being full members of society.

Poverty also brings with it a significant loss of basic rights and freedom; that is, it threatens our well-being as social and political agents. We know firsthand, again in disproportionate numbers, the humiliations that come from being subjected to a dehumanizing welfare system, and what it is to be subjected to the invasive and patronizing treatment of the social agents that represent and administer them. Welfare agencies are needed and play an indispensable role in supporting those who are poor. Without them the condition of the poor would be even more desperate. From a Hispanic point of view, however, for these programs and agencies to be effective and humane, it is important that those who are the recipients of its benefits play a more active role in its organization and policy making. This will contribute to and expedite the process of freeing welfare recipients from the dependency generated by an impersonal and bureaucratic welfare system. It can also give the program particular insights into the kind of assistance and interventions needed to solve the problems the poor confront.

At present, the political mood of the nation is defined by its attempt to reduce significantly the scope and impact of the welfare state and the various entitlement programs supported by it. Hispanics are suspicious of these and similar proposals because they are aware that, while it is true that these programs are not the solution to the poverty and paternalistic behavior their community is subjected to, without these programs and entitlements their condition as a minority racial and ethnic group would be worse. If the federal government gives local states the authority to determine the need, breadth, and depth of these programs, the condition of the poor and marginal, who are also the politically weak, will probably worsen. Although it may be true that people at the local level know best what is good for them, it is also true that the states have a long and painful history of not picking up and following through with programs aimed at assisting their weakest members. Many Hispanics, for example, believe that if the federal government had not pushed hard to enact civil rights for African Americans and for women, the states would have delayed the process of overcoming race and gender discrimination, denying justice to these discriminated-against social groups. Hispanics distrust overcentralization and accumulation of power, but at the same time recognize that there is a need for centralized power to ensure that all citizens receive their due. That is why, in general, we support federal entitlement programs.

SOCIAL OPPRESSION

Oppression and domination also manifest themselves within the present social divisions of labor. Hispanics perform many menial tasks that are not only poorly compensated, but what is even more significant in terms of one's sense of dignity and worth, that deprive them of the experience of exercising authority, having and carrying responsibility, and being recognized as contributing members of society. Too many among our people are mere followers whose lives are lived in obedience to the directions and visions generated and given by others. We not only occupy a disproportionate number of unfulfilling and boring jobs, but also are deprived of experiencing the joys that come from being consulted and having our opinions and concerns solicited and taken into account.

The predominance of nonwhite ethnic groups in menial jobs also contributes to the creation and credibility given to distorted social stereotypes used to describe who we are. We are seen by the dominant social groups as people who lack ambition, a work ethic, creativity, and imagination. Members within the dominant groups perceive and treat us as socially incapable and inferior, and beyond having distorted opinions about us, they also engage in equally distorted habits and attitudes toward us.

POLITICAL OPPRESSION

Although poverty accounts for much of the personal and social suffering experienced by Hispanics, it is neither the only nor the main cause of their being an oppressed social group. Political powerlessness remains a more significant cause of the oppression we experience. At present we have some influence in state politics and within our communities; but we have minimal political voice and influence in determining the national destiny. We are too dispersed and still lack the necessary institutional infrastructure and the networks needed to engage effectively the national political agenda. This is a condition that subjects most Hispanic communities to various forms of political abuse of power.

Our status as citizens is reduced to the act of merely obeying laws we did not participate in formulating. The laws and rules that guide the nation and significantly affect our lives are experienced as alien and tyrannical. We agree with the dictum "Power corrupts and absolute power corrupts absolutely," but we experience this dictum from the underside. In our view, "Powerlessness corrupts and absolute powerlessness corrupts absolutely." Powerlessness deprives us from exercising the necessary countervailing power to make dominant groups accountable and responsible.

CULTURAL OPPRESSION

Cultural imperialism is another distinct and probably the most universal and evident form of oppression experienced by Hispanics. Whenever the values and ways of life of a particular social group claim to be universally valid and essentially good, they also tend to become the norm of social acceptability and social inclusion. As a corollary of this claim, the values, culture, and ways of life of other social groups are seen not only as being *different* but also as being *deviant*. The cultural particularity of nondominant social groups is not *recognized* as different, but it is socially and politically *ignored*. This is why, within our dominant Anglo Saxon cultural setting, the struggle for communal emancipation carried out by the various racial and ethnic groups has cultural consciousness-raising as an integral part of it. Every ethnic group must struggle to enable its own members as well as other social groups, in particular the dominant social group, to come to recognize, understand, and respect the significance and importance of its own ways and views.

One experience shared by Hispanic migrants is that, when we live within our homeland we are treated by others as persons—equals among equals. When we transport ourselves to the United States, a painful transformation occurs: We become a minority. We are seen as people who lack something that only the culturally dominant group can provide, be it language, opportunities, a new way of living, or new ways of relating. We are defined as "other"[3] and deviant from "the right way of being." To remedy this lack, from the point of view of the dominant culture, we must be assimilated and resocialized into the right way, that is, the way of the dominant group.

The description of Hispanics and other groups as ethnic minorities is a "social construction" that cannot but become an affront to one's *dignity*. Day after day Hispanics live with the indignity of watching their culture, language, sense of beauty, and way of life devalued and criticized as inadequate. They are seen as culturally inferior and lacking adequate sources to derive meaning and direction for their lives. We become painfully aware that as minorities, no matter what we have done or achieved, we are still not fully accepted by the dominant group. The dominant culture, through the use of negative stereotypes, attitudes, and gestures, expresses the kind of suspicion about us that makes us doubt our own skills and talents.[4]

Even wealthy and powerful individuals within the Hispanic community are not free from the experience of indignity entailed in cultural imperialism. Some Hispanics who have "made it" engage in acts of self-hatred and self-loathing. In the hope of finally being accepted by the dominant social groups, some feel pressured to distance themselves from their community. We come to believe that maybe if we put distance between ourselves and our own kind and abandon our ways, we might be treated as an equal, a peer, or a fellow citizen in the full sense of the word. In extreme cases some even engage in acts of cultural denial, acts of insensitivity, mistreatment, and even meanness toward members of our own ethnic group. In "making it" we are not only physically uprooted from our communities but also left spiritually bereft and empty. This is at the heart of the Hispanic resistance to individualism and, in what could be interpreted as a countercultural act of resistance, why we hold on to our traditional commitment to communal life and communal solidarity.

VIOLENCE

Finally, oppression points to the fear and constant threat of violence that falls upon Hispanics by reason of poverty, race, language, or ethnic origin. We are forced to endure the violence that comes from living in ghettos and inhumanly impoverished "communities."[5] Most Hispanics do not yet enjoy the right to live wherever we choose. Many neighborhoods, for reasons of racial and cultural discrimination, remain closed to our people. And many financial institutions create obstacles, denying us the resources we need for the pursuit of business projects or to build our ideal home. Banks and other commercial institutions flee from and refuse to invest within our communities, which are the ones that need them the most.

There is also the wasteful and genocidal violence at the root of gang activity present in the streets and in the schools our children attend. The institutional, legal violence of our judicial processes accounts for the disproportionate numbers of Hispanics mistreated by the police, incarcerated, and placed in detention centers. Hispanics, together with other racial and ethnic minorities, are sentenced more frequently and receive harsher sentences than Anglo Saxon criminals. But the most insidious of all forms of violence is that unprovoked and random violence whose sole purpose it is to humiliate and degrade us simply because we are Hispanics. All of these manifestations of violence are at the root of the violence experienced within the family itself that particularly victimizes children and women.[6]

In light of what we have mentioned, one of the contributions Hispanics can make to the moral point of view of North American society is to make it more conscious of the fact that not only individuals but social groups are essential to the development of one's moral point of view. Social groups, as people who share a common history, language, religion, and social identity, are instrumental not only in shaping our moral character, but also in enabling us to understand and interpret the morality that informs their lives. From a Hispanic perspective, humans do not exist for ethics, but ethics exists for enhancing the goodness of our life together. What this entails is that the needs of people have priority over principle, familial and group relationships are morally more significant than abstract conceptions of justice, and the moral systems of subcultural groups are normatively more relevant than universal standards of ethics.[7] What we represent morally is the occasion and commitment for our society to become truly multicultural, genuinely inclusive, and radically compassionate and caring. Our ethics is based on caring for the powerless and poor; it is an ethics of love for a society that is increasingly loveless and unable to give hope to members within it who are worse off. Our ethics calls for recognition and respect of difference and for empowerment of the various social groups that constitute our nation, as the best way to make the claim "justice for all" a concrete, lived experience.

We can identify three dominant moral concerns in the language Hispanics use to articulate our moral points of view: a commitment to moral principles, a concern with character formation, and a quest for group recognition and care. Each of these concerns gives rise to a particular style of moral reasoning: the ethics of principle, character ethics, and the ethics of recognition and care. My claim is that these three styles of moral reasoning contribute to the eclectic way Hispanics engage in moral reflection. It is also my claim that the ethics of recognition and care is gradually becoming the predominant, but not exclusive, way Hispanics articulate their moral point of view.

The Moral Points of View of Hispanics

Let us begin our journey into Hispanic moral reflection by examining the main traits, strengths, and weaknesses of each of these styles of ethical reflection. To do so I will analyze a recent movie, *Mi Familia* ("My Family"), produced by Francis Ford Coppola and directed by Gregory Nava, which narrates the history of three generations of a Mexican American family in California. The story depicts the migrant journey of the father (José) from Michoacán, Mexico, to California, the unjust deportation of the mother (María), and the many vicissitudes they live through with their six children. This popular and entertaining movie contains a number of scenes that quite vividly describe the various ways Hispanics interpret and respond to the moral dilemmas they confront. I will focus mostly on two scenes particularly germane to our depiction of Hispanic styles of moral reasoning and our concern with the issues of identity and dignity. Again, my aim is not to provide a solution for the moral dilemmas presented in these scenes, but rather to point to the dominant motifs found in the language by which Hispanics express their moral views and commitments.

MI FAMILIA, SCENE 1: JIMMY GETS MARRIED

This scene takes place at the end of the movie. Jimmy, the youngest of six children, is now a man. He has served time in jail for armed robbery, is not employed, is single, and still frequents his parents' home. The narrator of the movie, Paco, the oldest son, also a bachelor and an aspiring writer now engaged in writing the story of his family, relates that all family members were ashamed of Jimmy. However, in Paco's view, the anger, rage, and sense of injustice that fills Jimmy's soul freed and enabled all other members of the family to live more normal and productive lives. Jimmy's anger comes from witnessing the murder of his brother, Jesús (Chucho), by the police. Like Chucho, Jimmy is a mean *bato*, a rebellious young man with a mean attitude fed by the awareness that beyond his family he has no place where he belongs and that the society in which he lives neither cares about nor loves him. He dwells in a kind of social limbo, affirming a different way of being that is given little recognition and respect. He lives between two cultural realities: the Mexican heritage of his parents and the Anglo world that expects him to cross the bridge to find work, but which never itself crosses the bridge to come to his community. He does not fully identify with either of these cultural worlds.

One day, while watching wrestling matches on TV and fixing a lamp for his mother, Jimmy receives a visit from his sister Antonia. (Antonia used to be a nun but has recently married an Anglo priest she met while they were both doing mission work in Central America. When she told her Catholic parents about her marriage the mother fainted and the father could only say, "If it's O.K. with God, I guess it is O.K. with us.") Antonia and her husband are community organizers and advocates for Central American refugees. Antonia's visit is not social; she comes with the intention of asking Jimmy for a special favor. She shares with him a case she is presently working on. There is a woman called Isabel, a refugee from El Salvador, who has been picked up and arrested by the Immigration and Naturalization Office or la Migra. She is illegally in the country and is going to be deported. What is worse, once returned to El Salvador she will either be put in jail or, in all probability, killed. Isabel has not been politically active, but she is

the daughter of a union organizer. She witnessed the way the Salvadoran military regime killed her father.

Antonia tells Jimmy that she and her husband have a plan to free
Isabel. If they can only show that Isabel is engaged to be married to a
U.S. citizen, they can delay the extradition procedures and obtain her
residency and eventual citizenship. Jimmy replies that the idea is no
good, that "the Migra could not be so dumb." Antonia says that he
would be surprised how dumb they actually are. The real problem is
that they need the volunteer this day. Jimmy laughs and tells her that
he doubts that they can get a *baboso* (nerd) citizen to marry this girl on
such short notice. In glancing at her, it becomes clear to him that
Antonia is not just sharing her worries with him but that she is asking
him to be the "baboso" prospective husband. Jimmy, quite upset,
refuses: "Marriage is out of the question." Antonia emphasizes to him
that a life is at stake, to which Jimmy replies, "Yes, my life is at stake."
Antonia retorts that her request is no big deal, just a matter of signing
a piece of paper, no babies, no commitment, just going through some
legal motions to save a girl's life. But Jimmy holds firm—"marriage is
out"—and recriminates against Antonia that ever since she was little
she has been "bossy, always knowing what is best for everybody," a
"control freak." Sensing she is losing him, Antonia tries a new tack; she
tells Jimmy that both of them know that "the system" is for s___, and
that this is his opportunity to say "f___ you" to the whole establishment. "This is your way of getting back at all of them, cops, judges,
guards; the whole system." He is still resistant and then Antonia hits
him in a vulnerable spot. In a tone that questions his machismo, she
challenges him: "If I was a man, I would do it."

In the next scene we see Jimmy with his sister, brother-in-law, and
Gloria (the Anglo woman who contacted Antonia and in whose house
Isabel works as a maid and child-care provider) at the Migration office
to free Isabel. Once out, they all go before a justice of the peace. During
the private ceremony, after the papers are signed, Isabel approaches
Jimmy for the traditional kiss, but Jimmy withdraws from her and
starts to leave. As he leaves Jimmy jokes that he will be back next week
to sign the divorce papers. Antonia congratulates Jimmy, tells him he
is amazing, to which Jimmy replies, "You owe me." Antonia and her
husband hug each other in celebration, rejoicing and shouting "we

won, we did it again!" And there stands Isabel quite confused about all that is going on, confused and dazed, while she is hugged and kissed by Gloria and everyone else celebrates their own private victories.

That evening all family members and Isabel are at Jimmy's parents' home. Everyone is quite nervous, pacing back and forth. Isabel, still confused and somewhat afraid, asks Jimmy's mother, María, "Please help me. I got married today . . . where am I supposed to go, where is Jimmy?" José, in a tone that reveals how upset he is, asks Antonia, "What were you thinking of?" At that same moment Jimmy walks in the house and seeing Isabel he turns around and says, "I have something to do, I will be back later." His mother stops him, tells him to come in, and asks him to explain what is going on. Jimmy responds, "pues nada" (nothing). "¿Nada?" his father asks. "This girl says you are her husband; is that true?" Jimmy replies, "Technically speaking, yes, but it is not really true," telling them it was all Antonia's idea. Antonia, quite defensive, replies, "Is this the Spanish Inquisition? We saved her life," and defiantly exclaims, "Maybe someone should thank us." The father tells both of them, "You always know what is right for everyone with your porquería política. Did you ever ask Isabel what she wants?" Antonia interrupts him, "What do you mean what she wants, we did not have time to ask." The father continues, "You just messed up this girl's life without asking her permission." Antonia insists "they [the Migra] were going to deport her, without asking her permission, and when she got out of that plane they [the Salvadoran army] were going to shoot her without asking her permission. . . . Maybe we should have left her alone and she would be dead, all nice and neat."

Then the mother intervenes: "You young people, you think no one has ever lived before you did. No one knows anything except you! Do you think I don't know what it feels like to be picked up by la Migra, about the dangers of being deported, separated from your family, not knowing what will happen? Do you want to tell me something about survival?" (María speaks with authority; she was illegally deported when she was pregnant with her third child, Chucho, and sent back to Mexico. She took a painful journey back home and almost drowned with her son when she attempted to cross a river.) Looking at Antonia she tells her, "Certain things are sacred, 'Sagradas,' and we don't spit on them, because without them it does not matter whether we live or die. Marriage is something we do not spit on, and Isabel believes she is married."

Memo, who is about to become a lawyer, tells Jimmy, "You said those two little words, you signed a legal document; the law believes you are married, too." Jimmy replies, "The hell with the law. That was a political action; I am a goddamn revolutionary," and instructs Antonia to explain to Isabel that he will not see her again and leaves abruptly.

THE ETHICS OF PRINCIPLE

Some Hispanics express their moral views in the legalistic or judicial language characteristic of the culture of modernity. This is particularly true of those Hispanic Americans who aspire to be fully assimilated into this society. But it is also true of all of us, insofar as we cannot escape the influence of the Anglo Saxon moral tradition embodied and dominant in the basic social institutions under which we presently live.

Those who abide by the ethics of principle focus on human action and decision making. Their main concern is to determine the right action we are obligated to perform. In this style of ethical reflection one proceeds by formulating general and abstract principles that are universally binding and to which we can appeal directly, or are embodied in rules as guides of action and judgment. Thus, legally and morally speaking, if it is true that acting in a particular way is right, it follows that it is always right to act in the same way under all similar circumstances. Memo, the lawyer, consistently assumes and articulates this point of view in the movie. His reply to his brother Jimmy, who is trying to minimize the moral significance of his decision to marry Isabel, is that he said "those two words [I do]" and that he signed a legal document. Jimmy acted out of good intention to save Isabel's life, a morally praiseworthy goal, and in signing the marriage license he also made a promise that is legally binding. For Memo, obeying the law overrides Jimmy's subjective intentions of doing good. Obedience to the law is morally binding in the most stringent sense of the word, and one of our main moral obligations. Thus, in Memo's view, Jimmy must fulfill what he promised. For the ethics of principle, promise making and promise keeping are not to be taken lightly, no matter how one feels about them. Morality must be justified on something other than our desires, our economic, political, or ethnic interests, our religious convictions or cultural traditions. Only reason provides a universal and objective valid justification for our moral principles, and this foundation is what makes it possible for all rational creatures to recognize them as valid. Memo is a representative of those Hispanics who, while having empathy to understand people's feelings, needs, and concerns, attempt to keep a spirit of detachment and objectivity when it comes to considering the moral thing to do.

Hispanics who accept the ethics of principle hardly ever abide by a single moral principle; we tend to appeal to a plurality of principles as guides for action and judgment. Even though, like most people, we would like to have absolute moral principles that apply with no exceptions, we are realistic enough to recognize that, under the conditions of human existence, we cannot avoid making exceptions. It is clear to us that, at times, equally valid moral principles come in conflict and we cannot help making exceptions. However, if there are no absolute moral principles, we must recognize that not all exceptions are morally valid. The only legitimate justification for us not to abide by a particular moral principle, is that we intend to comply with an alternative but equally valid moral principle.

Antonia, and to a lesser degree Jimmy, could have replied to their brother Memo (Antonia does so indirectly), that they, too, acted on the basis of principle: the moral principle of saving the life of the innocent. They accept Memo's claim that obeying the law and keeping our promises are part of our moral obligations. However, when the laws are unjust, that is, when the laws do not protect or seek the well-being of all citizens, and threaten the life of the powerless, they can, at times, be overridden by other moral obligations, such as the obligation to preserve the life of the innocent. For Antonia this is the case with the laws of immigration regarding Central Americans.

If for Memo there seems to be no higher standard than the law itself, for Antonia laws and principles in themselves do not automatically solve our moral quandaries. In order to know what the right choice is, we must take into account whether or not there are relevant circumstances that call for a different moral response. In her view we must assume a discerning attitude, and at times we must be flexible enough to decide against our presumptions and moral preferences. For Antonia the immediate challenge and task is to protect Isabel, the asylum seeker. She would consider doing almost anything to make sure that Isabel is not sent back to El Salvador. And given the urgency of this circumstance, it is justified to lie and disobey the law, not because these lack moral value, but because they are overridden by the principle of saving the life of the innocent. Antonia was able to persuade Jimmy to join her in this act of disobeying the law on the grounds that he, too, has experienced how principles and laws formulated by dominant groups are used to dominate and abuse the poor and marginal.

Antonia could also make the case that even though Isabel is in the United States illegally, she still deserves to be protected. Her presence in this country is due to the policies of repression and murder of a government and military force that is supported by the U.S. The United States is morally responsible for both the flow of refugees and for arbitrarily and unfairly closing the border to refugees and migrants who do have legitimate claims to being admitted into the country. (Gloria, the naive but well-intentioned American woman, cannot believe her country can do anything like that.) Not to take into account this political dimension of Isabel's dilemma is to distort the interpretation of what is happening and to provide an insufficient moral response.

Given the conflict of principles and the urgency of the case, Antonia chooses saving the life of the innocent over the equally valid principles of truth telling, promise keeping, and obeying the law. She recognizes that moral principles are not to be taken lightly and that they are more than advice and counsel. Principles are morally binding, but not absolutely so. They are normative guidelines that can be overridden, but only by other equally binding moral guidelines.

Hispanics realize that the plurality of moral principles we use to guide our actions and judgments are neither unrelated to nor independent of one another. Principles are intrinsically related to one another and constitute themselves as a cluster of mutually dependent values. The moral institution of life necessitates that we make a serious effort to abide by and honor the demands of all the principles. If, in our moral choices, we always disregard one particular principle, or if we always show loyalty to the same principle, the danger exists of jeopardizing and undermining all of them. The moral institution of life entails juggling and weighing principles with the intention of honoring the diversity and richness of our moral configuration of values. Insofar as both Memo and Antonia decide to disregard each other's value claims, they both risk losing something significant to the moral institution of life. If they recognize each other's claims and merely disagree as to what is the preferable course of action, they live within the tensions of the moral life but do so in a way that respects and, thus, ultimately preserves its integrity.

To the central question raised by the ethics of principle, "What should I do?" two answers are possible: (1) Do that which will bring the best consequences and minimize harm for everyone involved, or (2) do that which is right in and of itself, independent of the consequences of your actions. Those who give the principle of beneficence and utility priority in their system of values advocate the first mode of ethical thinking. Those who give autonomy priority choose the second.

THE PRINCIPLE OF BENEFICENCE AND UTILITY

Consequentialists argue that the morally good is determined by the ends, outcomes, or consequences of our actions. What are "good or worthy ends" is variously defined by individuals and groups. For some it is pleasure and consumption, for others the development of reason, spiritual pursuits, friendships, or the contemplative life. Whatever the end, consequentialists determine the morally good action by how that action brings about or denies us the end we pursue. Both Antonia and her husband work from a consequentialist mode of thinking. They are mostly concerned with identifying challenges and goals, and fashioning responses that would lead to the realization of the ends they pursue, for example, allowing refugees to find asylum and to stay in the United States.

Consequentialists also differentiate themselves from one another by the weight they give to moral rules. Some take what is known as an *act* or *situation ethics* approach. For them, each particular case or situation is different and unique. Moral rules are reduced to counsel that we are free to disregard in light of the demands of the unique situation in which we are called to act. It is the unique situation, not the rules of promise keeping and obeying the law, which dictates what we ought

35

to do. This is the way Antonia argues her case. The urgency of the situation leads her to lie and make her brother lie in order to save an innocent life.

Others, however, argue that the principles must be embodied in general rules that serve as stringent guidance posts. Moral rules are stringent and take precedence even when, in a particular situation, they will probably not bring about the greatest good. *Rule teleology* as this alternative is called, takes into account what has proved to work, and focuses on the long-term consequences of our actions. María questions and challenges Antonia's situationalism. She argues that given what we know about marriage, what Jimmy and Antonia have done will, in the long run, be damaging to Isabel *and to all of us.*

In María's view, the sacredness of certain things must not be violated even if doing so brings short-term good consequences. One of the problems with Antonia's solution to Isabel's dilemma is that in her passion and zealous commitment to saving Isabel's life (which is not pure since she also wants to stick it to the government and la Migra), she loses sight of Isabel's feelings and wishes. Antonia is so focused on the immediate situation that she fails to consider the long-term consequences the fake marriage will have for Isabel and Jimmy. Jimmy also assumes a very short-sighted approach and short-term perspective. What is worse, Antonia borders on acting in an immoral way, since she seems more interested in her mission as a refugee advocate than in Isabel's well-being. Jimmy, who claimed to be a "revolutionary," ends up mistreating Isabel through his initial avoidance and rejection of her. If Jimmy had stuck with his basic intuition that marriage is marriage, that is, that marriage matters, he would probably not have done what he did. Antonia remains unrepentant of her actions and believes them to be the best. Jimmy's running away shows that he is aware that what he did, even if it had good consequences, remains morally suspect.

Overall, Hispanics, such as María, prefer the rule mode to the act or situational mode. The situational mode, while having the advantage of making us sensitive to the uniqueness of each situation and freeing us from dogmatism in our moral interpretations and responses, remains too arbitrary and time-consuming to be practical. Most of us recognize that when we engage in moral deliberation we are not always capable of being in the same serene mood and clear state of mind, nor do we have the energy to consider afresh every situation in which we must make a moral decision. In our view rule teleology is more "energy efficient." Rules allow us to learn from the accumulated experience of our ancestors and our culture and religious tradition. They also allow us to teach the wisdom of our past to our children. Thus, moral rules are significant to us in that they connect us meaningfully with the past and project our responsibility for the future.

Consequentialists tend to lift up the principles of beneficence and utility as normative for our actions and judgments. Hispanics recognize that we have a moral obligation to contribute to the goodness of others' lives. We believe that just because we derive benefits from the network of social relationships we dwell in and from the contributions made by members within our comunidad, we owe others our contributions to the well-being of their lives. We express this commitment through the acts of hospitality we extend to friends and strangers, and through loyalty to family and our ethnic community.

Beneficence and utility are maximizing principles.[8] Beneficence expresses the ideal that we ought always to do good and never do wrong. Utility is a compromise of this ideal; it obligates us to choose, from among the alternative actions available to us, the one that will bring about the greatest positive good and the least undesirable consequences. The simplicity and common sense nature of these principles makes them inherently attractive, since it seems intuitively true that we have a moral obligation to minimize evil and, whenever we are able to do so, to contribute to the goodness of our lives and the lives of others. Antonia believes she has saved Isabel's life, which in her view is the greatest good she can do for her. When she compares all other alternatives, she might accept that what she did was not perfect, but insists that no better alternative was available or preferable to the one chosen.

Beneficence is a conditional principle, since we can only be obligated to contribute to the well-being of others if it is possible for us to do so. Whenever we (1) are aware of someone in a state of need, (2) have the resources and skills necessary to act in ways that can satisfy that need, (3) can act in a way to make a difference in the person's life, and (4) can assist the person without undergoing undo sacrifices or disrupting our life plan in any significant way, we have a more stringent obligation to benefit such groups or persons. One might want to do good beyond what is morally required. However, for the most part one is not morally obligated to contribute to the well-being of others when one is not able, or when so doing significantly impoverishes one's life prospects. All of these conditions are mentioned by Antonia as she tries to persuade Jimmy to agree to marry Isabel. As a last resort, when it is clear to her that all rational arguments are failing, she appeals to his base instinctual feelings, his machismo!

For many Hispanics, however, rule and act utilitarianism has drawbacks that prevent us from making the principle of utility our exclusive or dominant criterion of moral action. Utilitarianism tends toward *the end justifies the means* kind of thinking. It disregards the significant moral differences that exist between two actions and attitudes if both actions bring about similar consequences. If we can achieve better consequences by either lying or telling the truth, both actions are seen as morally equal. Utilitarianism neutralizes the differences between these two kinds of acts, but this is counter-intuitive to the moral sense of most Hispanics. These considerations are at the heart of José's and María's recriminations against both Jimmy and Antonia. For both of them there are right ways and wrong ways of solving problems; therefore, not all means justify good consequences.

It also fits the utilitarian mode of thinking that a social group or individual bracket or sacrifice personal interests in order to improve the general well-being of society. In ways similar to oppressive notions of sacrificial love harbored within the Christian community, utilitarianism can support practices and policies that call for even higher levels of sacrifice from those who can ill afford them, all in the name of the common good. There is one sense in which Isabel's interest is sacrificed and is used to make a political point that will, it is hoped, benefit future refugees. The fake marriage definitely enhances the confidence of Antonia and her husband to continue to advocate for the refugees. At the wedding ceremony, they celebrate their own personal victory in beating the system. Isabel, on the other hand, is not aware that there is a good reason to celebrate, and she has good reason to resent being used without her consent for someone else's well-being.

THE PRINCIPLE OF AUTONOMY

The other answer given to the questions, "How do I determine the good?" and "What should I do?" is, Do that which, independent of its consequences, is, in itself, right. This nonconsequentialist, duty-based perspective claims that there are factors more significant in determining moral obligation than the outcome of our actions. Our duties and obligations are determined by the inner traits of our actions themselves. And doing what is right takes precedence over achieving the good.[9] For example, murder, torture, and rape are actions that in themselves are always wrong, no matter how desirable or positive their consequences could be. The same is true of lying, breaking a promise, being unfaithful, or faking a marriage. The terms used to describe such actions already signify that it is wrong to do them. On the positive side, the terms "truthful," "faithful," and "honest" describe actions that are in themselves desirable, and thus it is our duty to perform them even when they do not bring forth convenient or good consequences.

María and José represent this mode of ethical thinking. Marriage and the promises and commitments it brings are good in themselves. As such, they place us under obligations that cannot be taken lightly. Lying and faking marriages are actions that in themselves undermine the integrity of our being and the possibilities of living in community. In María's words, certain things are "sacred" (and as if to show how sacred they really are she emphasizes using God's language, ¡Sagradas!). She goes on, "We don't spit on them, no matter if we live or die." Of course it does matter whether we live or die; but the mother wants to make the point that not any means justify the end. She undermines her daughter's consequentialist bent by questioning her capacity to predict consequences. In María's own case, who would have predicted that she would be unjustly deported to Mexico or that she would be able to overcome the risks and challenges she confronted in her return home. There is no way we can predict the consequences of our actions. It was the sacredness of marriage that gave her an incentive to come back. María and José find it quite disturbing that the value Isabel places in the act of marriage has not been respected, and that Antonia and Jimmy did not recognize Isabel's state of confusion as an evil.

María's response to Antonia is an example of the Divine Command Theory, which is a religious expression of the ethics of principle. Scripture and the church provide us with a list of rules and principles that we must follow both to be saved and to live upright moral lives. Religious fundamentalists approach the Scriptures in this spirit. Of course Antonia could have replied that the Bible also provides for acting according to the principle of beneficence. The biblical story of the good Samaritan and some interpretations of the love command provide Hispanic Christians with a prototype and rules that beneficence entails. Stories like this one call one to be attentive to and contribute to the well-being of others, in particular the weak and helpless. They motivate and inspire us to cultivate attitudes of helping others and to make them an essential part of our day-to-day lives.

Antonia believes that since she and her husband probably saved Isabel's life, the actions they took to achieve this desirable end are good, or at least not morally reprehensible. Circumstances emerged that justified her doing something that is usually perceived as wrong. Most of us, to some degree, can sympathize or agree with Antonia. We might condone lying if so doing would save the life of an innocent party. Even María might agree. Still, María's ethic of duty makes her stress the point that lying and disobeying the law, in spite of their good consequence, are morally wrong. The goodness that we achieve through bad acts does not eliminate the fact the we have transgressed something which is significant to the integrity of our humanity and to the possibilities of living within caring and loving communities. Such acts themselves reveal the brokenness of our communal life and doubtfully contribute to enhancing the integrity of our being. If we must do such acts, we should at least recognize that they are morally wrong, express and feel remorse, and engage in acts of contrition. Repentance and contrition become more stringent obligations for the religiously inclined. That her daughter, a former nun, does not confess and admit the wrongness of her actions is as disturbing to María as the wrongness of the actions themselves.

There are drawbacks to the ethics of duty that remain a concern for most Hispanics. By exclusively focusing on what is right, it can become insensitive to the obligation we all have to enhance the good. That is, at times this mode of ethical reflection refuses to raise what, for

Hispanics, is a morally significant question: For whose good is this action taken? Hispanics look for and work in hope for a better future, a future where a fuller life will be accessible to more members of society. Always acting out of an uncompromising sense of duty can lead to dogmatic and cold forms of behavior that disregard its possible negative consequences. Too many Hispanics have been victimized by what has been claimed as an absolute moral principle—principles, of course, formulated without our participation and which do not really include us among those they protect and serve. This danger is present in María's claim that sacred things are never to be violated, "whether we live or die."

Duty-based morality theories emphasize the principle of autonomy and the language of rights. Hispanics, like other racial and ethnic minorities, find the language of autonomy and rights attractive because it signifies our longing for freedom at the heart of our struggles for justice. Autonomy and the language of rights are attractive to Hispanics because we sustain a vision of a society truly blind to differences that have traditionally been used to justify discriminatory forms of behavior against our people. Although we will always debate whether there are such things as universal rights, one has to note that the language of rights has national, cross-cultural, and international significance. It has become an acceptable and frequently used language in international relationships and of movements committed to progressive social change. Antonia could have appealed to the language of universal human rights to argue her case to protect Isabel. This language is accepted within our political establishment, our religious communities, and other influential centers of power.

The language of autonomy is at the root of the Hispanic understanding of human dignity. A person's dignity is intrinsically intertwined with her or his being a creative agent with the capacity for autonomous decision making. Dignity demands that we be allowed to live in light of self-given rules and consulted in all matters that affect our lives in significant ways. Whenever Hispanics feel that their point of view is not taken seriously or when they feel treated in a paternalistic manner, they use the language that their dignity is being violated.

Autonomy is at the root of José's complaints that no one has asked what Isabel wants, and it is the basis of his reproach of Antonia for assuming what is good for Isabel without asking her. María also lifts up the principle of autonomy when she points out to Antonia that "Isabel believes that she is married," that for Isabel this is a matter of much importance and value, and that no one has bothered to show respect or take Isabel's value system into account. Both parents resent that her children have treated Isabel as a child, and that they have not made her part of the decision-making process. Antonia and Jimmy have violated her autonomy and rights and taken advantage of the fact that she is in a social context she does not understand. The fact that Isabel might not be competent to defend herself legally and politically in the United States does not, in the parents' view, justify her not being consulted in matters relating to her marriage.

Within our political culture, the language of rights and the principle of autonomy are biased toward the protection of individual interests. Rights promote social arrangements that protect individuals from undue interference from others and, in particular, from the political State. They serve as moral entitlements that empower individuals and safeguard their capacity for self-determination. The principle of autonomy promotes the conviction, in a way utilitarianism cannot, that no person should ever be made a mere means for the benefit of others, thus depriving that person of dignity.

At present in our society we have both positive and negative rights. A positive right entails the obligation, as a matter of justice, to assist our fellow citizens. Positive rights place us under the obligation to do something for another in order to satisfy a socially specified need. Certain needs must be satisfied so that individuals are not harmed in ways that seriously impede their capacity to be autonomous agents. Negative rights, on the other hand, create safety zones that enable people to pursue their interests. They place on us the obligation to refrain from intervening in other people's lives. Our society, particularly in this last decade, has a bias toward negative rights and an inclination to minimize, in spite of the existence of the welfare state, the proliferation of positive rights. Hispanic moral language, however, expresses the opposite priority. We believe that assisting the poor and satisfying their needs is a moral imperative that has priority.[10]

In conclusion, Hispanics affirm the principles of beneficence and autonomy. We disagree among ourselves as to which of these principles ought to be given priority, but we do not question their moral relevance. We keep both these principles in tension and balance the demands each places upon us. They do not save us from the need to engage in careful reflection and discernment of what seems to be the fitting thing to do. They do not in themselves solve the moral dilemmas we confront, but they do make us aware of those significant elements that we must take into account as we strive to act in a moral manner. These two principles define the moral differences between the various members of the Sánchez family. Those like the parents who give priority to the principle of autonomy, do so because they are convinced that to focus too much on the language of beneficence and providing assistance can create among the needy a social consciousness of being mere victims, or passive recipients of the generosity of others. It makes the needy overdependent on the goodwill of others and deprives them of the joy of knowing and experiencing that they are agents capable of shaping their own destiny.

Others, like Antonia, choose the principle of beneficence because they are convinced that the condition of the needy and powerless will deteriorate significantly if there are no programs, organizations, or individuals willing to provide whatever assistance is needed. In their view, to promote self-reliance is a legitimate moral end, but not at the risk of allowing an individual or social group to drown in the oppression and domination with which they are victimized. Hispanics like Isabel are not victims, but too many of our people are victimized in various ways. For Antonia, one has the obligation to assist people as a necessary step in the process of empowering them to become agents of their own destiny.

It is important to point out that the characters within this movie who assume the language of rights and autonomy do so in an apolitical manner. They seem to be oblivious of, in part because they are suspicious of, the political and social implications of the principles of autonomy and rights. In preserving individual freedom, the principles allow individuals and social groups to be critical of the status quo and to initiate a process of social reform that can contribute to the common good. They serve justice by enhancing our awareness of the need to create democratic political structures that provide protection against oppression, intolerance, unequal treatment, and economic domination.

And they create a space where free public discussion and decision making are at the center of our common life. The connection between the language of autonomy and rights with the language of self-worth and self-respect merges the concerns of autonomy with those of social justice.

However, the strong commitment Hispanics have to family life and their sense of loyalty to their ethnic community necessitates a moral language broader and more comprehensive than that provided by the ethics of principle in both its consequentialist and duty-based modes. The principle of autonomy and the language of rights, though valuable, remain too cold and impersonal to the Hispanic way of being. It is a language proper for people who are essentially unrelated to one another and who meet in the public square as strangers who are equal and free in socially significant ways, to negotiate, assert, and affirm their interests and rights. Its individualistic bent also makes it quite indifferent to group rights, for example, the rights of cultural identity that are at the center of the ethical concern of Hispanics and other racial and ethnic groups.

The Hispanic focus on intimate relationships and our sensitivity to the needs of others cement our conviction that we have moral obligations beyond those defined in terms of rights and impartial universal laws. Within the family and the comunidad it is not the language of beneficence and utility, nor the language of law, rights, and contracts between free agents that makes moral sense, but the language of commitment, mutual dependence, care, love, and compassion that communicates what is morally required. In these contexts obligation and responsibility take precedence over rights.

CHARACTER ETHICS

The moral language used by Hispanics expresses moral concern with issues other than moral obligation and decision making. For many of us the root cause of the lovelessness and violence our comunidad must confront day-in and day-out reveals an individual and collective defect in moral character. This signifies a commitment to character formation and the development of moral virtues among our people.[11]

Character ethics focuses secondarily on our actions and primarily on the character traits of the moral agent who acts and chooses. It is concerned with the kind of person we become as we choose and perform particular acts. When Jimmy calls his sister a "control freak and bossy," he is pointing to what he considers to be one (not the best) of her character traits. The same is true when María and José complain that Antonia seems always to know what is right for everyone. The family reveals to us Antonia's inclination for and her character trait of jumping in with both feet before she carefully considers the consequences of what she is going to do. Since Jimmy is considered by the family a "screw up," no one is particularly surprised that he consented to fake a marriage; this is part of who he is, a person inclined to defy authority. It is this element of Jimmy's character that in all probability made Antonia believe that she could get him to consent to her scheme. Of course Antonia reveals many positive character traits: compassion for the needy, persistence and imagination to do what she considers just, and a deep love for her family and those she identifies as capable of being family members.

In this style of moral reasoning, the development of a virtuous character is morally more significant than mere conformity to rules and principles. Rules can always be avoided, while a strong character has permanence and reliability. People of character do not just follow rules or merely abide by an external sense of obligation; they are internally disposed to do what is morally right, particularly when the going gets tough. They act out of a firm and unchanging state of character and, what is equally important, harbor within themselves the right state of emotion and desire. People of character show a kind of consistency of being that leads to the creation of a coherent story. From the point of view of character ethics, the ethics of principle and autonomy have the inherent danger of basing moral decision making on free agents whose choices can become arbitrary.

José and María frequently narrate to the children their individual stories in order to show them what it means to be a good person. José narrates and, like all good storytellers, has a propensity to exaggerate the dangers and challenges he confronted in his yearlong walk from Michoacan to California. His story reveals the values and virtues of loyalty, mutual aid, and love of family. He recounts the many vicissitudes he confronts on the way, and the courage and consistency of purpose required to undergo and accomplish such a journey. And he shows pride in the struggles he has undergone to support and provide for his family, which for him is the most important thing in the world. María narrates the challenges she confronted when she was illegally sent back to Mexico and decided to come back home. Her story is also one of courage, initiative, commitment to family, and unbridled capacity for unselfish love.

The parents value character because persons of sound moral character are more likely than others to understand what should be done, more likely to perform the acts that are required, and even more likely to envision and act on moral ideals. In this perspective many of the moral quandaries we confront, and the inadequate way we respond to them, reveal that problems lie not in not knowing what to do, but in lacking the character and the virtues necessary to address them. Furthermore, when people of sound moral character commit a wrong act, as all finite and sinful creatures are prone to do, when it is pointed out to them, they will be predisposed to correct it. The fact that Antonia does not recognize that what she is doing is wrong is particularly disturbing to her parents precisely because it points to a character flaw. That Antonia undermines the sacredness of marriage is disturbing not only because it is a wrong act, but mainly because she is becoming the wrong kind of person, even worse, the wrong kind of Catholic.

Hispanics committed to character formation do not disregard the focus on action and decision making central to the ethics of principle. They do make the language of moral obligation secondary to the language of character formation, but the intrinsic relationship that exists between these two types of ethics is affirmed. To a great extent, who we become is determined by what we do, and what we do is shaped by who we are. When one examines the language used by both ethics, their affinity and correlation become quite evident.

Principle ethics stresses the importance of *acting* under the guidance of the principles of autonomy, beneficence, and justice, while character ethics calls us to *be* respectful, benevolent, and just. The virtues of truthfulness and faithfulness are developed to some degree by abiding by the principle of and doing acts of veracity and fidelity. Although different in emphasis, the ethics of character and the ethics of principle are seen as ultimately compatible and mutually reinforcing. These two styles of ethics are necessary but different dimensions of the moral institution of life. Therefore when asking a virtuous person: What ought I to do in these circumstances? we must not be surprised if he or she responds: "I do not know!" One cannot assume that a person who displays a virtuous character will always act in morally acceptable ways or always know what to do. People who are properly described as virtuous commit morally unfit acts, either because they were ignorant of a significant fact, made an honest mistake, or did not have the skill to make their actions effective. We will always need principles to help us decide what to do, particularly when we must choose between conflicting virtues, and we will also need to learn how to move from principle to action. Principles are indispensable guides of conduct, and knowing how to apply them is a skill and an element of the moral life we all need.

Every time one of their children does something José and María consider wrong or troublesome, they wake each other up in the middle of the night and wonder what it is that they did wrong. The narrator of the movie tells us that if it were not for Memo, the upcoming lawyer, the parents would never be able to get to sleep. Both parents believe that they have provided their children with a good moral example and a nurturing home. They know they have modeled to their children what it means to be loving, caring, disciplined at work, and committed to improving the well-being of the family. They wonder why all this modeling and storytelling has not rubbed off on their children.

Moral virtues are those cemented, internal dispositions, intentions, and inclinations that reveal our commitment to acting according to the demands of moral principles. They are character traits that we have had for a long period of time and which are consistently manifested in our habits of acting. Dispositions are attitudes of our temperament that have become settled within us. Intentions are related to our will or volition to pursue certain purposes and aims. They both give direction, stability, and even predictability to our behavior or conduct. They stabilize not only our actions, but also, and more important, our motivations and inclinations to act. To be a person of character is to have knowledge of the good and the inclination to act according to it.

Motives are also at the center of the ethics of virtue even though principle ethics tends to disregard them. When friends respond to our needs, we expect them to do so not merely out of a cold sense of duty or strong sense of rational obligation, but also with care and with a feeling of love. We want them to do what is right and to help us, but more important we need to know that their motives and desires are also proper. Their assistance should be accompanied by corresponding feelings of friendship and love. The friend and loved one who acts merely out of duty is hardly ever identified as a friend or a lover, because they are devoid of something vital to the moral institution of life.[12] The apostle Paul expresses this point of view when he states that it is not enough to do good or right acts, but that it is also necessary to do them with the right motive. "If I give away all my possessions, and if I hand over my body so that I may boast, but do not have love, I gain nothing" (1 Corinthians 13:3). If one performs the right action and acts out of duty, but lacks the proper moral motivation, neither the act nor the person is virtuous. One thing which all the members express to Isabel is their concern with her well-being. They all love her and care for her even though some of them may have acted in improper ways. That Antonia and her husband celebrate their victory more than show concern for the future of Isabel, reveals that they are capable of *acting* in insensitive ways, but not that they *are* insensitive persons.

The virtues are not natural to our being; they require hard work and need to be consciously cultivated over a long period of time. Abstract principles provide neither a proper source of moral instruction nor a proper spring for moral inspiration and action. Morality is learned in the doing of moral acts. It is best learned by watching and imitating the saints or heroes, those persons who represent the best values and moral ideals of the traditions and communities we belong to. Mentors and role models, supported by well-structured educational interactions, are indispensable to character formation. José seems to believe that he and María have been to their children like the broken corn he plants in his *milpa* (corn patch). The broken corn, when mixed into the soil, penetrates the growing corn, feeding it, giving it life, and making it erect and strong.

The individualistic bent of principle ethics and the language of human rights is alien to those Hispanics who look at morality from the perspective of character formation. Life in comunidad, and the quality of communal life, is perceived by us as an indispensable element of our moral upbringing. The language of character formation is attractive to us because of its emphasis on community life and the power our communities have in shaping our character.[13]

In the film, the main community that shapes the moral visions and characters of its members is the family. María and José make it quite clear that there is nothing more important than the family. But they have difficulty recognizing how their society, with its prejudicial practices and structures, its ideology of individual success, and market forces that encourage the values of meaningless sensuality, conspicuous consumption, and social and geographic mobility, seriously compromises the formation of moral character.

With the exception of Antonia, all the other members of the family lack an understanding of how the social world that surrounds us determines the kind of person we become. What the family really lacks is awareness of the importance of being politically committed in order to create a wider context of love and care that will influence the lives of their children and all the children within the community. The family is only one community that shapes who we become; there are many other communities within society that also influence the way we form our character. Most members of the family are apolitical or antipolitical and refer to political issues as "la porquería política." Part of their suspicion and their view of politics as "a big pile of garbage" is based on their isolation from and lack of understanding of the political process. They are isolated from the main decision-making centers, which are, as the narrator of the story tells us a number of times, on the other side of the *many bridges* that separate the Anglo and Mexican American communities. They do not see how much of what affects their family is the result of how power is organized and distributed within society, how they are the victims of cultural discrimination, economic exploitation, and an oppressive division of labor.

Thus, Hispanics concerned with character formation stress the importance of the quality of communal life and the preservation of tradition. Communities shape our vision, influence the way we look at the world, and give us a sense of meaning and of the goals we ought to pursue. They structure and define the roles and responsibilities we are obligated to perform, the goals we ought to pursue, and the standard of excellence by which we evaluate them. Traditions, which are also given, not constructed, provide us with a unique language, symbols, and systems of meaning. More emphatically than the ethics of principle, the ethics of character emphasizes the fact that we become who we are through relations with the world and others.

Both Chucho and Jimmy embody and live the consequences of their loveless and careless society. Chucho rebels against the Anglo world with the same passion; he rebels against his Mexican roots. Only the countercultural Pachuco culture he creates and lives in, dominated by violence and various degrees of self-hate, provide him with something like a community. Jimmy, inclined to petty crimes and with no sense of ambition, purpose, or direction, also embodies the anger and hatred that comes from knowing that one is not cared for or loved by those who have power over us. It takes the son Jimmy and Isabel conceived, the beginning of a family, to give Jimmy a sense of meaning. Memo, at least indirectly, reveals to us how modern corporations and the process of social progress significantly contribute to the breakdown of family life, neighborhood stability, and the experience of stable and close relations among family, friends, and citizens. He finds himself denying and domesticating his cultural roots in order to fit within a culture it is never clear he really belongs to or that will fully accept him. These negative forces are aggravated even more by the lack of commitment by social institutions to provide alternative and effective communal programs to overcome the detachment of individuals from their community and traditions. In the movie we witness commitment to promoting the values of caring for and serving the needs of others within the family and a diminished public commitment to the common good.

There is no such thing as an individual morality. There is no such thing as a universal morality applicable to all human beings and relevant for all circumstances. Morality has a particular and incarnational quality about it. To understand any system of moral rules and obligations we have to understand the community that lives it and the roles we are called to play within it. To grasp the fullness of meaning of a particular moral point of view we must, to some degree, attempt to immerse ourselves into that community's history and conception of the good life. Notions of the virtues and the good are internal to a structured communal life. We learn and know what we are called to do on the basis of our familiarity with a particular communal tradition, which educates us in all matters pertaining to the morally fitting and good. The quality of the communities we belong to, for better or worse, shape us in significant ways.

This is why Hispanic Christians claim that participating within a church is an essential part of what it means to become a Christian. Becoming a Christian and acting morally in light of this tradition requires continuous training and encounter with other Christians who can teach and model the *way* for us. It is not enough to read about Christianity or frequently talk about it; it is necessary to be in touch with the disciples or saints of the church and all those who, being part of the faith community, contribute to the preservation and growth of the religious tradition. The Christian community of faith provides the context out of which we engage in moral reflection and practical moral decision making. When we make a moral decision we make it representative of the faith community we belong to. This community provides the resources, that is, the stories, symbols, traditions, visions, and interpretations of God, self, and world that ground our choices. The community of faith informs and shapes in significant ways what we are and are not able to do. María, as we shall see, is the churchgoer and the one who has the most developed theological point of view. As she confronts the challenges of her life, her deportation, the murder of her son Chucho, and her disappointment with her children, she always has a theological or mystical explanation for them and finds comfort, courage, and hope in her religious heritage.

For all the emphasis on community life, Hispanics are aware that character formation is bidirectional. If it is true that our world shapes us in significant ways, it is equally true that each person has the capacity and the power to choose among the elements within society that we allow to influence us. We have the capacity to change and re-create the world that has been given to us. It is in this dynamic interaction that moral character is formed. In a very true sense we create and choose our own character as we contribute to the re-creation of the social and natural world. Jimmy, for example, while victimized by his social world, is able to redirect his life by the end of the movie by means of the same love his family provided for him. He makes a choice to change who he is and to live a new story. Paco, Memo, Chucho, Antonia, and Irene (the older sister who became a successful businesswoman), though equal members of this close-knit family and raised within the same neighborhood, all choose different ways to respond to their world and make decisions that shape the unique persons they become.

The significance of being framers of our own character is that we are never only victims. We must assume responsibility for the moral quality of our individual actions and of our social world. The social structure in which we live can channel our actions in a given direction. An evil and unjust social structure can make us act in evil and unjust ways in spite of our good moral character. An evil structure is a powerful reality, as Paul makes us aware; within society one encounters powers and principalities that make us act contrary to our best intentions. Thus, moral evaluations and concerns have to be directed not just to individuals and their characters, but also toward the social structure that defines the roles and responsibilities we are called to perform and which limit our choices.[14] This is at the heart of Antonia's community organizing and advocacy, and it is the reason why, for an increasing number of Hispanics, structural transformation is becoming a central and urgent moral matter.

Character ethics is attractive to many Hispanics because it promotes the creation of communities of moral conviction and mutuality that are instrumental to helping us live the morally good life. But there are dangers to this kind of ethics precisely because small, intentional communities with a strong sense of identity are not without moral problems. They can generate tribal and provincial attitudes and can make our moral concerns narrowly focused and self-enclosed. Internally, they can oppress and obstruct rather than become a means to the realization of our unique individuality; they can diminish rather than enhance our creativity. Externally or publicly, intentional communities can encourage separatist attitudes and diminish our social responsibility and contribution to the common good. To be morally evenhanded, intentional communities need help in taking distance from their particular interests, beliefs, convictions, and commitments. They need to find ways to be more objective and impartial when dealing with strangers.

This is one of the reasons behind the Hispanic commitment to the ethics of principle and individual rights. Rights give strangers a voice and empower them to demand recognition. In one sense Isabel is a stranger to the Sánchez family, and still they all recognize that she is entitled to their help and protection. The language of rights can enable us to relate to and include strangers in our field of moral concern and, in so doing, create occasions to initiate new relationships. And whether or not these occasions result in new intimate relationships, as happened in the case of Isabel, they do make us aware of the importance of contributing to the larger community. If the central question of virtue ethics is the determination of those communal values and traits of character that sustain community, then it is important to emphasize that the protection of rights is a significant way to promote communal values. Rights provide protection against unscrupulous behavior, promote orderly change, and enhance cohesiveness in communities. They allow diverse communities to coexist peacefully within a single political state. Even if life in community is the best kind of life, it ought not to weaken our individual goals or truncate our individual rights. All of these are the reasons why the Hispanic commitment to character formation is accompanied by a commitment to clearly defined and widely propagated basic political rights.

THE ETHICS OF RECOGNITION AND CARE

It is my claim that our moral language points to an alternative way of thinking morally, which I am calling the ethics of recognition and care. In my view this is the preferred, though not exclusive, way Hispanics articulate their moral point of view. It promotes values deeply ingrained in Hispanic culture and reveals something essential about the morally good life. For most of us: (1) The needs of people have priority over principles; (2) humans do not exist for ethics, but ethics exists for enhancing the goodness of our life together; (3) familial and group relationships are morally more significant than abstract principles and conceptions of justice; and (4) the moral systems of subcultural groups are normatively more relevant than universal standards of ethics. Hispanic ethics is predominantly an ethics of care for the powerless and poor; it is an ethics of love within a loveless society that is significantly less able to allow those culturally different members within it to realize their hopes. All of these motifs are central to the ethics of care and recognition. Hispanics, intentionally or unintentionally, embrace the ethics of care because we are aware that it protects and empowers us to be the unique people we are. It is a mode of ethical reflection that has as one of its primary concerns the transforming of the conditions of oppression and domination experienced by our people.

As the ethics of principle stresses what is to be done and the ethics of character focuses on who we are, the ethics of care emphasizes the creation of nurturing communities that empower us to become creative agents. In a manner similar to the ethics of character, the ethics of care views small communities such as the family, the church, and the creation of social and political voluntary associations as being central to the good moral life. These smaller and intentional communities provide meaningful spaces for the kind of intimacy and solidarity which cement a person's identity. These communities also provide a sense of membership and belonging, recognition and respect to all members, the assurance that basic needs will be met, and the assurance that no one intends to harm us but rather that all have goodwill toward us. More important, such communities protect the individual and the group from the tyranny of the State.

Care ethics has an inescapable political dimension that even Hispanics who are not politically militant cannot avoid or help being influenced by. It is a politics of compassion and love in which the responsibilities we owe one another are not defined by or limited to the rights individuals can legitimately claim. Hispanics find in the language of rights a spirit of litigation and conflict that does not easily fit our conception of moral obligation. We question the assumption made by the ethics of principle that moral responsibilities are the product of contractual agreements between free and autonomous individuals. For us, morality is mostly unchosen and socially given, and our ethical responsibilities must be extended to others that are essentially unequal, powerless and dependent. Moral obligations emerge from within our very concrete contextual attachments, like those found in family life, and are best expressed through the more familial language of satisfaction of needs and prevention of harm. Our duties, thus, cannot always be formulated as abstract rights or in juridical-legal language, as the younger son Memo, the lawyer, is inclined to do.

Politically speaking, the ethics of care advocates creating a wide plurality of voluntary organizations each independent from the other and focused on particular issues. It also advocates establishing ever-more-inclusive networks of mutual aid and assistance among these organizations. This commitment to solidarity among different communities is what distinguishes it from the ethics of character that is inclined to be more separatist and exclusive. Autonomy within a particular sphere of influence, and interrelationship in structures of solidarity and mutual aid, represent the dynamics of its social and political vision. As it argues for the creation of autonomous spaces for each voluntary association, it argues with equal passion for the promotion of more spaces where different groups can encounter and engage in dialogue with one another and arrive at a more sophisticated mutual understanding. It affirms the obligation to recognize and honor the differences among distinct groups, to create structures of mutual obligation, and to do so requiring a minimum of shared values and sociopolitical homogeneity. It is a politics truly committed to cultural and political pluralism.

The ethics of care and recognition attends to the concerns about preserving the identity and well-being of Hispanic Americans as an oppressed racial and ethnic group. It is committed to strengthening our social and political power so that we can become more effective political and social agents. It seeks also to redefine what is valuable work and to restructure the social division of labor so that Hispanics can also experience the joys of leadership and authority within the workplace. And it ensures a space for us to live in light of our culture and traditions as these have been handed down to us and redefined by us. Care ethics affirms a different vision of democracy, one that entails recognizing and preserving differences among social groups, and a degree of political and economic autonomy and empowerment so that each group lives in light of its vision of the good life.

As the ethics of principle adjudicates conflicts between rights, and the ethics of character faces conflicts between the virtues, the ethics of care must balance responsibilities owed the various moral communities that significantly shape our identity. Care ethics downplays the important universal rules, utilitarian calculations, and the principle of impartiality which are dominant in the ethics of principle and character. It is a group-based ethics. In a manner akin to the ethics of virtue, the ethics of care postulates that our identity is formed through the conversation and interactions we have with "significant others." As a formative element of our identity, one's cultural group is entitled to our preferential moral loyalty, and the needs of the group ought to be one of our primary moral obligations. Not to be morally partial to the groups that shape the unique beings we are, is understood as an act of betrayal. It is becoming alienated from and risking and severing relationships with those who traditionally have provided us with support. It is a way of weakening one's personal identity and one's social and political standing. If one's group also happens to be dominated and oppressed, the ethics of care stresses the importance of the practice of self-love. Self-love among the socially despised becomes a necessary condition for empowerment and their being able to move toward more inclusive social arrangements. Care ethics is our way of saying "no" to the forces that make us mere imitators and consumers of someone else's culture and way of life.

Antonia is the character who best represents the ethics of care in that she understands its political dimension. She is concerned, as her style of dressing, her speech, and her capacity to mobilize people reveals, with the preservation of the *cultural* identity of Hispanic Americans and Central Americans. She is *politically* committed to the empowerment of Hispanics. And she is *socially* concerned with their capacity to experience the joys of leadership and authority. She is the community organizer and activist, the one engaged in the "porquería política" (political "trash") that the rest of the family complains about. She feels an obligation to Isabel simply because she is Central American and is powerless. Her commitment to Isabel reveals her inclination to give preferential treatment to her "own kind."

However, Antonia's politics is not the politics of the establishment as defined by the State. She describes the State as being "f___ed up." Her politics is that of a community organizer who wants to empower a particular constituency, in her case Hispanics and refugees, and to limit and make the State more accountable and responsible to their needs. José and María also practice the ethics of care and recognition but do so within the private sphere of the family. They care for all their children and love them equally even though they are not always proud of what some of them do. Within their family, all members are brought up to have goodwill toward one another. The family works hard to provide a nurturing and caring environment for all.

For José and María the family is a safe haven and is the main community that provides children with the care and recognition needed to be morally sensitive and good. They slowly come to accept, although they never fully understand, that the care and recognition the family provides is not enough to sustain the self-esteem necessary for the proper moral formation of all their children. Their apolitical and socially uncritical attitudes make it harder for them to come to terms with the careless and loveless nature of the society in which they live, and the destructive power and influence this world has over their children.

Chucho was murdered by the police, who are supposed to serve and protect him; Jimmy, who witnesses the murder, is never able to let go of the anger or to cope with his awareness of the lack of love his world has toward his kind; and Memo, the one who made it, recognizes that he must renounce his cultural heritage as a condition of "acceptability" or "equal membership" within this world. Paco, the narrator, constantly denounces the divisions and tension between the east and the "pinche west side," where all the power, work, and opportunities for social advancement are found. He knows that the Anglo world can live without visiting his side of town, but that if he wants to improve his social standing, he must cross the bridge. Still, even Paco remains apolitical and chooses to deal with the oppression and domination of his ethnic group by means of cultural resistance. Irene, the restaurant owner who made it within her own community, is consumed within the private world of her business and family. She keeps elements of her culture, but also in an apolitical manner. Antonia remains the only one who is most aware of the need to struggle for justice and the creation of centers of power beyond the family, although at times her political style and passion make her overbearingly paternalistic.

For the ethics of care and recognition, the quest for freedom and equality central to the ethics of principle and character must necessarily go through the struggle for cultural affirmations and ethnic pride. With the exception of Memo and to some degree Chucho, all other members of the family take pride in their culture, in being who they are and sharing their unique stories. They are not all equally against assimilation, but all show signs of pain and disgust when they perceive that the price they must pay for integration is the surrender or domestication of their culture.

True freedom and equality need the retrieval and affirmation of our Hispanicity from the distortions Anglo Saxon culture presses upon us. Hispanics have learned that becoming *derivative* Anglo Saxons impoverishes their life and leaves it void of a viable system of meaning. Acculturation, in the way we have been forced to do it, has not and will not lead to acceptance by the dominant group.[15] Rather, it results in new opportunities for prejudice and discrimination. As members of ancient and honorable cultures, we cannot but be allowed to negotiate a dignified acculturation process based on mutual recognition and respect. Care ethics is a response to the apparent indignity and violation when we are defined not as persons but as racial and ethnic minorities, "other," "deviant," or people who lack or are less because of who we are culturally.

Hispanics not only have to be true to our cultural selves, which for us is a matter of dignity, but also must affirm our right to be recognized by others. In our present social context, recognition is not a matter of courtesy or etiquette, but something at the heart of the preservation of one's humanity and dignity. To be denied recognition is to be subjected to the domination and oppression of other social groups. It gives those who have minimal or no significant interactions with us the power to interpret and define who we are and what we can do. This subservience more than anything else, and the lack of care and love entailed in it, results in the formation and propagation of negative stereotypes of one's social group and way of life, and to feelings of low self-esteem (Chucho), rage and anger (Jimmy), and shame toward one's culture and being (Memo). If the process of integration is to open positive opportunities for all of us as members of this pluralistic society, we must, as Hispanics, care for the quality of life and well-being of our community.

Chucho is the only one who, in his struggle to re-create and redefine his own identity as a Mexican American, explicitly disavows his being a Mexican, and consistently demeans all things Mexican ("I hate that mariachi s____"). Yet, he has enough pride in his culture that he remains bilingual, cares for his family, and teaches the children of his neighborhood something very important: to dance the mambo! Memo's character, on the other hand, reveals a benign expression of the phenomenon of paternalistic acculturation. He struggles with the fear of not being acceptable to the Anglo community and, in particular, to the family of his Anglo fiancée. He is publicly ashamed of his family history, and in order to be acceptable to his future in-laws, he makes his parents deny many of their formative stories. The time he came to introduce his Anglo in-laws to his family he manifests his lack of comfort with the beans and corn that his father grows in his front and back yard. In his attempt to fit, Memo feels the compulsion to explain how his family's ways are similar to his Anglo in-laws' ways.

In its most extreme form, cultural paternalism and imperialism can lead to the distortion of self-esteem and even to expressions of self-hatred and hatred of other members of one's own racial and ethnic group. The inhuman consequences of lack of social recognition do not affect oppressed groups alone, they also affect the dominant group. They create among them false feelings and attitudes of superiority, aloofness, and disregard for the pain of those perceived as being less. When put together, these two factors create the conditions that lead to mistreatment and various forms of violent confrontation within and between social groups. And in both cases, our capacity to be authentic moral agents is significantly subverted.

Our identity and being is not only shaped in loving contexts, but also through the struggles against those who attempt to deny us our voice. Antonia's denunciation of the system as corrupt and f____ed up also reveals that she cannot afford to play by the rules of the system. In her view ethnic groups, in their quest for survival, have to devise their own ethical ways. Racial and ethnic groups cannot comply with the ethics of the system. To comply with the ethics of the system is to remain and accept domination and exploitation. Jimmy intuitively agrees with her descriptions of the system and with the need to have the alternative ethics. This, in part, explains her flagrant manipulation of the law of marriage and migration. Resistance to the system helps make possible our survival.

The ethics of care and recognition points to the essential dialogical nature of moral life. Dialogue, having a voice and the power to articulate genuine words, is at the center of what it means to be human and to sustain human life. We are very much the result of the conversations and interactions, loving and not so loving, we have with others. True conversation and dialogue require mutual recognition and equal standing. Care, which is essential for humanity to flourish, is based on communication. To enhance the possibility of greater mutuality we need spaces in which we can engage in dialogue from a position of relatively equal strength. The conversation between the in-laws is awkward because, although it takes place at the Sánchez home, they are still clearly at a disadvantage before the power and social prestige of the Anglo in-laws. The public power and prestige of one group is such that it dominates even within the private turf of the other. True dialogue requires the risk of opening ourselves to others and allowing them to influence the way we understand and experience our shared social world. Although Antonia and her father attempt to be honest in sharing their stories (Jimmy's jail time, their distant relative, el Californio, burial in their backyard, the journey from Michoacan to California), Memo makes them retract and deny them.

The lack of comunidad, of spaces of mutual recognition and care, generates among our young, but not only in them, disconnected and concomitant forms of destructive behavior.[16] Isabel, while being intimate with Jimmy, who finally decides to remain her husband, reveals to him her greatest fear: that she lives in a society full of people, but that no one knows her. She expresses the fear of nonexistence and invisibility that is part and parcel of the social condition of being alienated, marginalized, and deprived of public presence. Jimmy confesses to her that he, too, has the same fear and hurt. Both have experienced the cruelty of their society through the murder of a parent (Isabel's) and a brother (Jimmy's). Both experience the world as careless and not aware that they exist. This lack of social recognition, he argues, is the basis of his anger. Only after Jimmy *recognizes* Isabel as his wife are both of them able to share with each other that which matters to them. With Jimmy's phrase "I know you," a relationship of mutual support and love begins. These words allow them to share their pain, frustrations, and hopes, and to give each other mutual recognition and very soon to share a common, although brief, life together. One thing is strongly communicated in this movie, that one of our greatest longings within our present society, despite its riches and power, is the need for community.

The ethics of care emphasizes the fact that moral obligations take place between persons and social groups who are significantly unequal; some are powerful while others are vulnerable, dependent, frail. What the powerless and exploited expect from us is not detached respect for their rights, but emotionally attached attentiveness to their needs. In its zealousness not to be paternalistic and to abide by the principle of autonomy, the ethics of rights aims most of all at not being intrusive or violating the boundaries of other persons and social groups. In similar situations, the ethics of care finds an occasion for responsible intervention in the life of others. Feeling for and being immersed in the life of others, particularly in the life of the poor and powerless, is a way of establishing vital facets of the moral relationships. To avoid being paternalistic, as one intentionally and aggressively becomes involved in other people's lives, the ethics of care stresses the importance of justice as a moral principle.

This is at the heart of the debate between Antonia and her parents. Her parents complain that Antonia, assuming that she knows what is good for everybody, has ruined Isabel's life without asking her permission to do so. They argue for Isabel's right to autonomy, a right that ought to have limited the way Antonia dealt with Isabel's dilemma. In Antonia's view, given the circumstances of Isabel's case and the dangers involved in her deportation, it was not possible not to meddle in Isabel's life. She cannot accept her parents' recrimination that she arranged a marriage for Isabel without consulting her. Autonomy does not exhaust the limits of morality. What she did, while not perfect, saved Isabel's life from those who would have violated her autonomy in more significant ways. Antonia's commitment to refugees is such that, given their disadvantage and powerlessness, she gives herself permission to meddle in their lives whenever she perceives they are in danger or in harm's way.

By focusing on justice, the ethics of care disciplines and commits itself to acting *with* the poor and oppressed and not *for* them. It commits itself to the task of mutual consciousness-raising, organization and responsible participation in the re-creation of our social world. In this ethic, self-help programs and institutions are intrinsically tied to the process of cultural pride and affirmation. The poor and oppressed can become so immersed in their inhumane state of affairs that the danger exists that they begin to see and define themselves as victims. The focus on active involvement in the struggle for justice gives the poor and oppressed another matrix by which to define and understand themselves. They are not victims, they are oppressed; they do not depend on others for their emancipation, they, in solidarity with others, define themselves in light of their struggle for emancipation.

This dimension is lacking from Antonia's actions of advocacy toward Isabel. Her claim that there was no time to do so does not seem persuasive. Isabel could have and should have been informed of what was going on from the moment she was freed from the Migra. When Isabel tells Jimmy that nobody knows her, she can include Antonia among those who do not know her. Antonia, while genuinely caring for Isabel, does not recognize her as the creative, strong woman she is. Isabel's strength and resourcefulness are seen, as we are told by the narrator, in the fact that she was the only person Antonia could not boss around and in her making Jimmy accept being her husband. She is a woman who has been victimized, but who is not a victim. Given a chance, she can realize what she wants to achieve. Antonia is insensitive to Isabel's capacity for creative action.

Justice is central to the Hispanic ethics of care because it also saves it from becoming a justification for the ideology of self-surrender and self-sacrifice imposed on women by society at large. Hispanic women have made us aware how they have been forced into the task of being *the* caregivers and nurturers. Although this task is noble in itself, when one is limited to this social function and deprived of all other public functions, it ends up perpetuating the oppression of the caregiver group and sustaining the lack of recognition and respect already institutionalized within society. To some degree this is true for all the women in the movie, with the exception of Antonia and Isabel, who struggle against the social limits imposed on them.

The women in the movie are all strong characters, but quite accepting of traditional roles. They embody how sacrifice for the well-being of others is made into an ideology of self-enslavement and self-humiliation. It is the Hispanic women's struggles for self-affirmation that has created a clearer consciousness among all of us of the importance of self-love or legitimate caring for oneself as a condition of being better able to care for others. For the ethics of care, justice demands that all have equal access to the plurality of social tasks and the experience of being publicly recognized by others.

For too long, Hispanic men and women, but mostly Hispanic women living in the United States, have been forced to live their lives within the private realm performing tasks generally associated with cleaning and serving the household. Their life energy is spent serving others and following others' orders and visions. The focus on justice calls for a redefinition of the division of work, so that all workers who perform tasks that are socially useful have the opportunity to both follow and lead, to receive orders and to be heard with authority when they speak about matters important to them. José is rejected by Chucho precisely because of his passive acceptance of his social role as a menial worker. And Jimmy, while loving his father, also demeans the father's work as a gardener. Although the movie does not develop the theme in a full way, there are many occasions in which the father's role as a gardener or "lawn cutter" is seen as less than ideal.

Finally, the ethics of care and recognition, in a way that fits the temperament of Hispanic culture, emphasizes the importance of the emotional dimension of the moral life. Emotions and a spirit of empathy help us discern the circumstances of others and what their needs might be. The capacity to feel compassion, disgust, and outrage can be instrumental in our becoming morally accountable. On the other hand, attitudes of aloofness, indifference, and "out of sight out of mind," promote attitudes of moral irresponsibility. In stressing the importance of the emotional dimension, this mode of moral reasoning does not, in any way, minimize the role of reason and the need to be disciplined in our attempts to understand what is entailed in the situation to which we are responding. In spite of all their differences, all the members of the Sánchez family harbor feelings of care and true concern for Isabel and for one another throughout the movie.

The ethics of care attempts to be both biased and impartial; that is, it brings the need for contextual and passionate moral thinking by members of our group, together with a healthy dose of dispassionate consideration for people and groups different from our own. It shows loyalty for one's own and commitment to impartiality when deciding between conflicting, legitimate claims, both within one's group and between one's group and other groups. It argues from a position of intimacy while it recognizes that at times those who are different from us deserve to be judged more favorably. Even Jimmy, doing his best as a single parent, admonishes his overactive and rebellious five-year-old son that he has to behave and show respect when Memo's future in-laws are in the house. His son must do so just because it is important to Memo, and because they will soon become members of the family. The overall accommodation the family makes for their Anglo counterparts signifies their commitment to the care and recognition of strangers, and their willingness to give them the benefit of the doubt, since they, too, will become members of the family.

Among the dangers found within the ethics of care advocated by Hispanics are the tensions between the loyalties owed to society as a whole (the loyalty to promote national unity and a harmonious political community), and the loyalty owed to our social group. It recognizes that the politics of difference can encourage and promote a separatist mentality that is pernicious to social and political stability. It wrestles with the question of whether or not we can create a society whose members build the capacity to live in the tension between the communal need for some level of unity, and the need for greater group autonomy and differentiation. A related concern is the capacity of this ethics to allow its members to choose outside of the mainstream of the group. Can members question the traditional ways and give expression to their own way of being? Can the social group abide by and respect the right of its individual members to choose another way? Is there enough tolerance within the group to permit subgroups and critical voices inside? This is particularly relevant when we consider gender, class, and lifestyle struggles within a social group. The ethics of care can stress community life and loyalty to, and the intentional preservation of, tradition to the point that it can become chauvinistic and tend toward tribal and oppressive behavior both within and toward other social groups. It is important, thus, to raise the question of the inner tolerance of the community under scrutiny. This issue is given brief attention throughout the movie, but it seems that the family is able to remain reasonably open, both within itself and with others.

Dignity in the Moral Reflections of Hispanics

MI FAMILIA, SCENE 2:
CONFRONTATION BETWEEN FATHER AND SON

One afternoon, José receives a call from the police warning him that his third son, Chucho (which in Spanish means Jesús, as Bill means William in English), is suspected of selling drugs (marijuana). The father expresses his disbelief to the police, "No, he could not be involved in anything like that," but suspects it is true. That evening the father, who has been drinking (a sign that he needs to do something unpleasant), awaits Chucho's arrival. As soon as he walks into the house the father accosts him, asking him where he has been (a clear intrusion in Chucho's privacy). He asks him rhetorically if he has been looking for a job, to which Chucho replies "No" and shows him an impressive stack of bills, telling him that he has money. The father asks him where he got it and bursts out shouting "selling mota!" (marijuana). The father proceeds to tell Chucho that the police have called, in a tone of voice that reveals his respect for the police and for authority, and then recriminates that he did not raise a son to be a *sinverguenza* (a person without shame) *delinquente*. He reminds Chucho of the sacrifices and struggles he and his mother have undergone so that he can be a person of respect. Again he accosts him asking, "Do you have any pride?" and reminds him of the achievements of his sister Antonia (a nun) and his brother Paco, who is serving in the navy (now his voice really reveals pride). And then the father really gives it to him, pushing and grabbing him: And you're "selling marijuana like a hoodlum. . . . Do you have conciencia? ¿Tienes dignidad? [Do you have dignity?]"

Chucho fires back, "f___ la dignidad, f___ it! and f___ your struggle! You think anybody cares about it here?" Showing his father the stack of bills again he tells him, "This is all they respect here in this country, not la dignidad. It doesn't matter how you get it, as long as you get it." In an attempt to affirm his own identity, he tells his father he does not want to be a Mexican, pulling out weeds and cutting lawns, nor does he want to be like his sister Antonia (Toni) or his brother Paco. And looking his father straight in the eye he tells him defiantly, "I do not want to be like *you*." Punches now begin to fly, as if to accentuate the violence of the whole scene. The father hits Chucho in the face, and Chucho, younger and stronger, brings his father to the floor, but stops short of hitting him with his fist. Maybe it is the mother's constant supplication for them both to stop, attempting to make them aware that now is not the time to deal with this; or maybe it is Jimmy and Memo, his kid brothers, who are witnessing the whole ordeal as they cry their hearts out in fear; maybe it is some recognition of parental authority and respect for "el Jefe" (a way of referring to the father's authority as head of the family). Whatever the case, Chucho does not hit him. The scene concludes with the father's shout, "lárgate" [get out of here], a translation which falls short of expressing the rejection and intensity of the anger behind the command.

Paco, the narrator of the story, concludes the scene by pointing out that Chucho and his father cannot communicate; they live in two different worlds. For the father there is dignity in work. Paco adds that, on one level their father feels he is right in throwing Chucho out of the house, but at a deeper level it does not feel right.

Let us now reexamine how the different styles of moral reasoning interpret and judge various morally relevant dimensions present in this scene, in particular the sense of human dignity that permeates the moral reasoning of Hispanics.

José, the father, who many times assumes the perspective of the ethics of principle, does what he considers to be right. His sense of honor and dignity is revealed in his conviction that one must take responsibility for one's actions and that certain actions are in themselves right or wrong no matter what consequences result from them. He works hard to provide for his family, treats his wife and all children with respect and love, and keeps the promises he makes. To act respectably, with dignity, and with a proper sense of shame are in themselves right, even if one has to endure sacrifices in order to live by these principles. It is right to work for one's family, whether or not one's children appreciate what one does. It is right to serve one's country or to commit oneself to the church (to which José is not particularly close).

On the other hand, it is wrong to make money if one does not work, even worse to make money selling drugs. It is wrong to sell and use drugs no matter how much benefit one derives from such activities.

Such activities reveal a disregard for publicly recognized and legitimate authorities: the law and the police, as well as the moral mores of the family and the community. They also reveal disregard for others, reducing others to the status of being a means for one's petty benefit. Wrongful actions are to be punished just because they are wrong, and insofar as the son violates the principles of decent living that informs the household, the father is within his right to ask his son to get out of his house, even though it hurts him deeply to do so.

In this we can see that for José dignity is mostly an individual, personal matter. Dignity is something that dwells within us, part of what it means to be human, something no one can give or take away from us. In his view, even if others refuse to recognize our dignity, we still have it and can find ways and spaces to affirm it. Dignity is grounded in our capacity to make moral choices in the sense that we are a center of decision making. This is a democratic interpretation of human dignity. It assumes that all adult, sane persons have within themselves the capacity, the potential to make moral decisions. Dignity is related to our being moral agents, and as such, beings who have to be respected and given the space and opportunity to live their lives in light of their moral visions. This view of human dignity is foundational for the ethics of principle, the notion of universal human rights, equal citizenship, and nondiscrimination.

In light of what we have mentioned, it is wrong of the father not to listen to Chucho, to give up on him, and to attack him physically. The violent and disrespectful way the father acts toward Chucho, including reproaching him for not being like his other children, expresses his disregard for Chucho's autonomy and sense of dignity. In spite of all the wrong things Chucho has done, he still has dignity. And this ought to remain binding for him. Clearly Chucho's drug dealing undermines his dignity and the dignity and life prospects of those with whom he does business. The father has every reason to point this out and to refuse to accommodate himself to this lifestyle.

However, Chucho has the right of not wanting to be like his father and to refuse to accept the lifestyle of other members of the family. Chucho has the right to make wrong choices, including making lifestyle choices that are unacceptable to his father. His father has good reason to be hurt that Chucho expresses that he is ashamed of him and of his culture, but he has to allow Chucho the right to go his own way and define his own life.

In making his decision, the father appeals to principles and rules of dignity and responsibility, but shows himself incapable of placing himself in his son's situation. It is not clear that the father is aware of the pain and anger that Chucho feels toward his world. It is not clear that the father understands his son's struggle to form his own identity in a loveless world where racial hatred and violence prevail to such a degree that even a loving family is not enough support to contain the anger and frustration. José buys into the belief which is dominant in Anglo culture, that dignity is unrelated to one's race, gender, class, and national origin. That is, cultural identity is seen as irrelevant to human dignity. For Chucho, however, being an individual is being culturally bound, and affirming and being authentic to that cultural substratum is integral to self-respect. For Chucho, dignity entails not only being a center of decision making, but also being able to live in light of the culture and values we choose for or create by ourselves. This is why negative stereotypes are experienced as insults and real injuries to our personhood, sense of honor, and self-esteem.[17] Chucho is continuously confronted with an assault on and rejection of his Pachuco culture by his neighbors, the police, and even his family. For Chucho, ethnic groups and subgroups, in his case the Pachucos, must make their own moral judgments, which are particular to their social and existential situation.

The Hispanic sense that all are worthy of honor does not relativize the importance of one's cultural particularity, but emphasizes that all cultures have to be recognized and affirmed. For example, we claim that people in prestigious offices are honorable. We do so not because they are officeholders, but to signal that we admire their special obligations and responsibilities toward those who depend on their service. We honor officeholders because they serve the community. Honor is a spiritual force that links a particular individual, with her or his unique talents, to the community in bonds of mutual support and care.

José does not grasp the full meaning of Chucho's refusal to be content with a menial job or to be surplus labor. He does not hear in his words Chucho's awareness that he is denied the dignity that comes from having access to the productive process and being a productive member of society. The father seems to place all responsibility for what Chucho does squarely on his son's shoulders. He does not seem to care about the changing and hostile social world his son has been given to live in. He seems to assume that society is basically just, and he is blind to the many injustices, oppression, and domination to which Hispanics are subjected. José does not hear Chucho's complaints that the menial work that people like him are forced to accept, given the social division of labor based on race and class, deprives him of his autonomy, self-determination, and sense of being a moral agent.

Chucho has pride in being a Pachuco; this is at the center of his identity. He loves his younger brothers, his friends, and the members of his gang, and, in his own way, all other members of his family. But he is alienated from the world around him. As soon as he moves outside these small communities he feels threatened. His world is one in which the police view him as a hunting trophy and even fellow Mexican Americans will kill him merely because of the way he looks at them. The way he copes with his hostile environment is by assuming some of its worst characteristics. His life is organized on the basis of the most crude interpretation of the principle of utility: "The end justifies the means." Whatever generates money, the dominant social good that gives one access to most other social goods, is morally acceptable. In Chucho's interpretation of social reality, it makes sense to live by the rule: As long as one can make money, it does not matter how one does it.

At the end of this scene, the narrator tells us that the father is undergoing an inner struggle regarding the rightness of his decision to tell his son to leave the house. From the perspective of principle ethics, this is a conflict between rights. It can only be solved by determining whose rights have precedence: the father's right to live according to his moral values or the rights of family membership that entitle his son to live with the family in light of his own moral views and options.

Character ethics, as we mentioned, looks primarily not at what the agents do, but at who they are. The mother and father not only act responsibly and lovingly toward their family, but throughout the movie they reveal themselves as responsible and loving persons. The father's violent encounter with his son Chucho is really "out of character," while his mother's moderation, her consistent call for reconciliation, intervention for the sake of peace, and acute sense of timing (that is, her stating that this is not the time or the way to discuss these grievous matters), are very much *in* character. The father is not a violent man; this is not the way he relates to people around him. On the contrary, he is a well-mannered and shy person. But the reconciling, nurturing manner the mother assumes reflects the way she always relates to those around her. As we mentioned, the courage, consistency in commitment, goodness, faithfulness, and other-regard exhibited by the parents are part of their personal history or narrative, and serve as a good witness to the other members of the family. The father expects his children, in a manner similar to the corn he grows, to nourish themselves from their parents' narrative and example.

José is a Don, a person worthy of our respect. You can rely on him; his word is good. His personal dignity is not grounded solely in his capacity to make moral decisions; rather, it is intrinsically interwoven with the best work ethic and family values of Mexican culture. José's personal story is framed within the context of a larger Mexican narrative that takes pride in work, self-improvement, and in providing for family.

When the police call to tell José that his son is selling drugs, his reply is, "not my son"; that is, not a member of this household, we do not do that sort of thing, we are not that sort of people. The father's conflict and frustration with Chucho stems from the fact that he is the only one among his children who has resisted being shaped and formed by the values that give the family its particular character. This is what makes Chucho different from Irene and Paco. José, although in denial, suspects that Chucho has the kind of character that does not fit the family way. What is worse, he fears that it might be too late to change his character, which is why he kicks him out of the house.

Chucho has looked for models outside the family, and chosen to follow the narrative of other communities. This option is damaging in that Chucho is not only doing bad things, but is becoming the wrong kind of son, the wrong kind of citizen, and the wrong kind of person. His personality is being shaped by the values of conspicuous consumption, tantalizing pleasure-seeking, and violence in quest of dominance and control. He no longer even knows what dignity, shame, and honor are. Outside of love for his younger brothers and loyalty to his subgroup, acquiring money and the things money can buy are the only things that matter to him. If his father understands, and this is never made clear, that these alternative communities are the cause of Chucho's corruption, he still holds his son responsible for what he does and who he is becoming. He recognizes that ultimately it is Chucho who is responsible for the options he has made. In his father's eyes, Chucho is not a victim of his world; if he has been victimized he can resist and can, or could have, chosen differently.

At the time the father confronts him, he is convinced that Chucho cannot be redeemed by the family. In fact, Chucho expresses his shame and contempt for the family way. He no longer understands what are the virtues, responsibilities, and obligations of being a son and a brother. In his alternative community, the words "dignity" and "respect" have no meaning and precious little value. Thus, it is proper for the father to tell Chucho to leave. What is at stake is not only a conflict of principles and rights, but the danger entailed in the admiration which the younger brothers, in particular Jimmy, have for him. Chucho can model for them the wrong values and virtues, and could become a negative and damaging influence on their moral formation.

The father's violence, as we mentioned, is out of character, while María's continued commitment to family reconciliation is very much a part of who she is. María is clear that there are certain things we cannot do, not just because in themselves they are wrong actions, but mainly because doing them can significantly damage the kind of person we become. These are the things she calls "sacred values" and the things she sees as being tied to human dignity. To have dignity is to abide by the ways of God or the supreme being. Chucho just cannot hit his father. And his father should not have forced him to leave. These actions undermine the compassionate and caring dimension of our character and community, and open a greater space for resentment and anger to flourish. In the mother's perspective, there is always a possibility of redemption and new beginning. Forgiveness, the capacity which allows us to begin again and again, is a central virtue of her personality. It is what leaves open the possibility for us individually and collectively to have a better future. The actions of Chucho and his father, both their words and deeds, show how false courage and machismo override their sense of fidelity and compassion for each other. The mother wants Chucho to stay. In her view, if character cannot change at will, it can still be transformed by the power of love and compassion. She has a strong dose of the virtues of faith and hope: faith in her son's ultimate inner goodness, as seen in his loving care for Jimmy, and hope in the power of family life to bring Chucho back to the ways of the family. In this sense, dignity entails uplifting and giving a new sense of values to those who have been victimized by the status quo.

Jimmy, one of the younger sons, reveals a significant character flaw in his father. When Chucho is hiding from the police after knifing and killing a rival gang member, he asks Jimmy what his father said, which signals that he very much cares about what his father thinks about him. Jimmy responds, "Dad never says anything." The father had minimum skills and little inclination to communicate. He could not speak at his daughter's wedding, but honor compelled him to do so. Nor could he talk or listen to Chucho, thus the violent confrontation.

Still, the father's hesitation in making his son leave, as described by the narrator of the story, is another indication that this act does not fit the father's character. It reveals his continuing concern about his moral integrity. Given who he is, it would make more sense to have acted like María. Chucho needs continuous modeling of what dignity, honor, and the virtues of being a caring family member are. Only in this way can there be hope that sooner or later he will see these virtues as being better and more conducive to a humane and good life than the choices he has actually made. To continue to model for and confront Chucho with a different way of being is morally better than beating him or exiling him from the family. Still, the damaging effect Chucho can have on his younger brothers and on the family as a whole is something to keep in mind, and is something that can justify his expulsion from the family.

Finally, from the perspective of the ethics of care, the contradiction between different rights and the contradiction between different virtues are real and must be taken seriously. However, they are not the ground or center of the moral dilemmas experienced by different family members. The purpose of life, as the father claims, is found in building a family. The moral focus is on the emotional moral content of our actions and the qualities of relationships that take place within the family itself and the other significant communities. The family is the dominant community at the center of the formation of our personality, and thus of our moral character. What is morally significant is the fidelity, compassion, love, trust, commitment, and willingness to act on behalf of those with whom we have significant relationships. Dignity, thus, is related to our struggles to create and sustain communities of love and mutual care.

It is María, the mother, who is the ethical powerhouse throughout the movie. Every action she performs carries with it the right emotion and the right intention. She also acts out the strong religious conviction that the virgin watches over them and does not want bad things to happen to her family. Even when Chucho is killed, she knows he was on "borrowed time" since he should have drowned when, as a baby, he was carried away by the river currents. She is the one who best handles the conflicts of responsibilities that abundantly emerge within her family. She cares for her husband and child, so much so, that in the heat of the fight she puts her petite body between them. It is not her physical strength that contains them, but probably the authority her sacrifices for her family have won her, and the respect and the care all know she has for them. In the middle of the fight she not only pleads for postponement of the discussion (her husband has been drinking and she knows the anger her son harbors in his soul), but she also will be the source for reconciliation. She also has the capacity to intervene without taking sides with either of her family members.

It is clear to her that anger, resentment, and physical abuse thwart and might permanently damage the family. Such feelings and actions do not fit the promotion of positive, lasting relationships. Even worse, they make authentic recognition of the needs of others impossible. This is the problem with Chucho's gang activity. This community has its own morality and even a sense of honor, but in the end the tribalism and disregard for others fuel forms of anger and violence that are destructive to self and community. She knows Chucho is wrong, but she is discerning enough to be aware that he, probably more than any other of her children, needs to be helped. And for the love of her son she is willing to take the risk of keeping Chucho home. In a sense, she acts like the shepherd who risked ninety-nine sheep for the sake of the one missing. If all are not there, no part can ever be whole, revealing how, for her, emotional content is always tied to creating structures of mutual interdependence.

The father's strong sense of right and obligation is marred by his weakness in communication skills and care. Still, he is loving and capable of responsible commitments to others. He loves his grandson, Jimmy's son, but knows that the child, whom Jimmy at one point abandons to his care, needs his father. José loves him but still is willing to let him go. He can provide for the child, but believes that only the father can give the kind of love the child needs to become a man. José also knows that the only way Jimmy will himself become a real man is through the love he shares with his son. María is the main or purer caregiver, but the culture to which both María and José belong is based on care and responsibility, in particular, care and responsibility to one's dependent children. Thus, José cannot escape being influenced by it.

María and José share an ethical flaw upheld by most members of the family, a flaw which may be an identity trait among Hispanics: a deep distrust of political activity. As we mentioned, many are the times in which political activity is defined as "that garbage." They do not see the importance of creating communities of responsibility and care outside the family structure. Nor do they see how the absence of structures of love and care within society at large is at the heart of Chucho's claim that only money matters, no matter how one gets it. Only Antonia, the nun turned social activist, understands the danger of the injustice of their political world and the importance of creating for her people alternative social and political possibilities. José and María are full of love, but are disconnected from justice. It is Antonia who embodies and models a more comprehensive sense of dignity characteristic of Hispanics. It is she who sees the need to unite care and justice.

José and María do not see that the partiality they have for their children has to be extended to their larger social and political Hispanic community. This is necessary for the family to find a larger context of support for their loving ways, and for their children to find islands of care and security outside the immediate family. The political has to be made into a sphere in which mutual interdependence and responsibility are also found. Chucho's rejection of his father's work ethic expresses not his contempt for his father, whose opinion he cares about, but his contempt for his father's passivity and acceptance of his traditional role. Chucho understands about care, as he is caring toward the neighborhood's children, but longs for that justice that entails being recognized and respected in one's difference, which would allow him the space to be who he is. He might be the only one who understands that care needs justice if it is to overcome domination and oppression.

The family is aware of the low and subservient status they have in society. This is made acutely clear when Memo, the younger son, brings his blonde Anglo fiancée and her parents to visit his family. Memo is now the lawyer who made it! But at a price. He changed his name to William and, in the dialogue between the future in-laws, continually interrupts in ways that reveal his embarrassment with the family history and their behavior. Memo, in spite of his success, is embarrassed of being Mexican and has no capacity for affirming his cultural identity.

To lose the grounding of our unique social ethnic heritage is to lose honor and dignity. It is to be alienated, inauthentic, and thus deprived of the possibility of forming identity. The national drive toward a melting pot, which Memo buys into, particularly when it does not welcome every social group, is a threat to individuals' building a clear sense of identity and dignity. Dignity is related to the struggle to preserve and perpetuate our unique identity; it is related to fulfilling the longing for community, spaces of and for mutual recognition and the exchange of care. In their absence, our youth, like Chucho, will be victimized by destructive forms of disconnection and concomitant forms of destructive behavior.

In the next chapters we examine different ways Hispanics commit themselves to promoting social justice. This will expand on the personal dimension of ethics we have dealt with in this chapter. It will also help us examine the possibilities of this commitment within the formation of a new Hispanic American identity.

CHAPTER 2

STRUGGLES FOR SOCIAL JUSTICE AND THE PLURALITY OF MORAL VALUES WITHIN THE HISPANIC COMMUNITY

Introductory Comments

In this chapter we examine the diverse moral values that lie at the heart of different struggles for justice in which Hispanics are presently engaged to empower and emancipate their people. We believe these moral values are essential to what it means to be human, to live a good life, and to sustain a just community. They are the values that are intrinsic to our sense of human dignity and that are at the core of the process of redefining our identity as Hispanic Americans.

The fact that Hispanics uphold diverse and at times conflicting values has, as is to be expected, both positive and negative consequences. It allows us to constitute ourselves into well-defined support communities that are action-oriented and which share a strong sense of identity, direction, and meaning. However, diversity of value commitments in the absence of structures of solidarity and mutuality, has the negative practical implication of keeping the larger Hispanic community fragmented and in conflict. Thus, our internal value conflicts can have the direct or indirect undesirable effect of supporting the condition of oppression and domination under which we are forced to live.

My claim, which I will develop more fully in chapter 3, is that within our Christian religious heritage we have resources to overcome the negative consequences of upholding diverse value commitments. Our theological traditions empower and enable us to reinterpret and transfigure our interpretation of the values we uphold in ways that allow us to create structures of solidarity among ourselves, between ourselves

77

and other social groups, and to work in common toward the creation of a more diverse, inclusive, and compassionate political community. As we create new and broader coalitions, we will not only promote the well-being of our community, but will also provide a witness and new vision for the United States to become a truly multicultural, caring, compassionate, and inclusive society.[1]

Justice and the Hispanic Moral Point of View

The language of domination and oppression used by many of us to describe our living conditions in the United States reveals, explicitly or implicitly, our concern with justice. Before we examine the substantive meaning we give to the values that are intrinsic to justice, let us first make some general remarks about the nature and scope of justice. By adding justice to the principles of autonomy, beneficence, and utility we discussed in chapter 1, we will have a more complete understanding of the configuration of values that informs the moral point of view of Hispanics. It also enables us to understand better both the grounds of diversity in our value commitments, and possible grounds for moral solidarity between different subgroups and sectors of the Hispanic community.[2]

First of all, justice is usually understood as a distributive principle. The goal of justice is to secure for all citizens their fair share of both social goods and burdens. Hispanics recognize that the distribution of social burdens and benefits is a legitimate justice concern. Among Hispanics, however, the distributive focus, which is dominant in most justice talk, is rejected because it supports and gives the benefit of the doubt to the status quo that sustains our oppression and domination. Distributive notions of justice, for the most part, assume the adequacy of the status quo. When we limit justice to distributive concerns, we not only conceal the different ways the present system dominates and exploits us, but also how it places our need to affirm our group identity outside what is considered to be a legitimate justice concern. It is the social configuration of power, however, that determines who is more likely to be subjected to the dominance of others. Justice, thus, is secondarily concerned with the distribution of wealth, which remains a significant part of justice, and more focused on the issue of structural change seeking to empower all citizens to participate within all centers of decision making that affect their lives in significant ways. Justice also becomes concerned with the question of cultural emancipation, and the power to be able to live in light of who we are. Living in light of one's ways, and having a say in the determination of one's destiny, is what makes us tie justice with claims of human dignity.

Second, claims of justice emerge when groups of citizens, seeking to secure the goods they need to achieve those goals that give purpose to their lives under conditions of relative scarcity, press competing claims against each other. If scarcity were absolute we would lack the inclination to be deliberative about and lack the desire to comply with the demands of justice. If, on the other hand, goods were in abundance, all having access to whatever we need to realize our life plans, we would have a minimum of or no concern with justice.

Third, principles of justice apply mostly to the basic structure of society and the social practices that emanate from our basic institutions. This emphasis on the social structure is what makes justice essentially a political and social concern. Principles of justice enable citizens to be aware of their rights, their legitimate claims and expectations, and their entitlements and responsibilities due them as members of society. Justice concerns do not directly apply within our interpersonal or private interactions. This is why justice, though morally important, is not enough. We also need love, care, and compassion to sustain and nourish our more intimate relationships where most of morality takes place, and on which our commitment to justice ultimately relies. Still, many Hispanics are coming to the realization that justice must be part of family life, since within the family important social goods such as leisure time, decision-making power regarding the use of money, and cleaning and child-rearing tasks, are distributed.

Fourth, principles of justice, like all moral principles, have a substantive and a formal dimension. If, in a large public gathering we ask, "Who stands for justice?" almost every person, no matter their religious or political convictions, will probably raise a hand. If, however, we tell those gathered that justice entails either giving half of what they own to the poor, or alternatively, being left alone to accumulate and use their resources as they please, we will discover less agreement than before. While formally we all agree that justice is a relevant moral claim, when it comes to determining the material principles of justice by which we decide who is and who is not equal in matters of social entitlements and distributions, we have serious differences and frequently engage in heated debates. This is why, when we employ such commonly used terms as "justice" or "love," it is important to ask what exactly is meant. We cannot assume that we know what we are being told when someone says that he or she stands for justice.

JUSTICE STRUGGLES AND VALUE PLURALISM

Hispanics have chosen different spheres within society from which to launch our struggle to forward the emancipation[3] of our people and enhance the justice of our society. This has led us to formulate different, and at times competing, notions of justice. Our struggles for justice take place within the *political* sphere, the *social* sphere, and the *cultural* sphere.[4] Within each of these spheres a different hierarchy of values has emerged to order the configuration of norms and values we share in common. And different material or substantive meanings are given to the different principles that are seen as normative and which lead to the creation and maintenance of the just and good society.

POLITICS AS THE LOCUS OF JUSTICE

For many Hispanics the political sphere is the proper locus in which to engage in justice struggles and to work for the emancipation of their people.[5] Domination and oppression are first of all political conditions that must be addressed in political terms. For political activists, power has a primary place in their configuration of values since politics is primarily concerned with the creation, distribution, and accumulation of power. It is precisely the manner in which power is presently created or re-created, accumulated and distributed that keeps Hispanics and other racial and ethnic minority groups in a permanent position of disadvantage and submission, making it impossible for them to enjoy a good life.

In this view it becomes morally imperative that Hispanics organize themselves politically, in solidarity with other people of goodwill, with the goal of transforming important social institutions.[6] Nothing less than direct political intervention and the conscious exertion of countervailing power against the powers that be, will enable disadvantaged groups to open society to new possibilities that are more life-affirming for all its members. The political perspective tends toward a conflictual model of society and a confrontational model of social change. In this perspective the ruling or dominant system of values is neither universal nor the result of rational persuasion. Dominant values are not the result of social consensus, but the product of that uneasy truce and compromise that emerged from the struggle of different social groups attempting to defend and assert their interests against the whole of society.

This view is informed by a realism regarding the limits of moral suasion and the need for coercive political power to change unjust situations and to preserve a more just social order. Political and moral persuasion based on rational argumentation is recognized as essential to democratic life but is, in itself, an ineffective means to bring about the institutional changes necessary for our emancipation. Structural changes will come when Hispanics are able to accumulate and assert enough power to make others understand that it is in their interest to recognize and respond to our needs. To lack power is to lack a voice in the determination of one's being and to be threatened with social invisibility. And the dignity of a politically invisible and silent people will most likely be violated. Dignity, for us, has an inevitable collective dimension. We know that we are rejected not only as individuals but as members of a despised social group.

Politics, as power conflicts, is perceived by the political activists as a zero-sum game: The more others have, the weaker our position will probably be. And since this perspective assumes the position of the powerless, the question of accumulating power takes a tactical precedence over the concern with distributing power. For most Hispanics, the ideology of division of power and the systems of checks and balances, beyond their rhetorical attractiveness, do have substantive meaning and value. To keep the powerful accountable, power must be distributed. In a just democratic order it is indispensable that people be actively engaged in the processes through which the important social decisions of society are made and needed change is brought about. This militant engagement sustains a wide distribution of social, economic, and political power. Hispanics recognize the importance of keeping social, economic, and political power widely distributed. Many have been victimized by their former nations' long histories of absolute and unchecked power and the corruption and abuses this entails. One reason Hispanics immigrated to the United States was precisely to avoid such abuses.

For Hispanics and other powerless social groups in the United States, however, it is imperative to give prior attention to the need to concentrate power. This will enable us to become effective agents for social change, capable of transforming the present social configuration of power and of improving our life prospects. Otherwise we will continue to be significantly restricted from affirming our legitimate interests, and others will be able to assert an undue amount of influence over us and over society as a whole.

If absolute power corrupts absolutely, it is also true that lack of power corrupts all of us. A powerless group is left with no way to affirm or defend the goodness of its being. Our humanity and the possibility of a good life depend on our ability to acquire enough power to see that we have the resources and services needed to pursue it. Empowerment ensures active and effective membership, and the rights and possibility of carrying responsibilities and duties within the community to which we belong. These are essential elements for individuals and social groups to experience self-worth, fulfillment, and dignity.

However important power is for those of us who struggle within the political sphere, we recognize that power is not an end in itself. Authentic and liberating power is at the service of justice. In this perspective justice is understood primarily in political terms. Justice has to do with the creation of a community where its diverse social groups are equally empowered to determine the sacrifices they are willing to undertake to obtain their self-given goals. Justice has to do with the creation of social institutions that sustain a diversified but highly participatory community. In a just society, different social groups give themselves the occasions and spaces to establish bonds of solidarity with one another as they actively pursue what is valuable for them and what contributes to the realization of others. In a just social order, while we nurture our particularity, we are also able to share in each other's burdens and celebrate each other's joys.

In this view, the political dimension of justice is given priority over economic concerns. Clearly there are severely depressed areas or "communities" in urgent and critical need of basic material goods and services. Much of the suffering we experience is due to the poverty we are forced to endure. But we suffer even more from powerlessness, which prevents us from having a voice in the process by which the nation determines its destiny and from affirming our interests and goals as a distinct social group. The political has priority because only politically empowered social groups and an active citizenry can assure themselves of the resources they need to enjoy the good life. How the economic structure functions and who it serves or does not serve, is ultimately a political matter. Democratic political control and democratic forms of ownership support the wider experiences of community that make and keep life humane. Participating meaningfully in the creation of a diverse, pluralistic, while inclusive and compassionate community is seen as more important to being humane than to merely having more.

In this perspective, community is a more basic reality than individuality. Many of us accept the proposition that who we are is significantly determined by the communities we belong to. We see an organic connection between our individuality and our character-defining social groups, a connection that entails special moral loyalty and care for those who contribute to our unique way of being. Among the greatest injustices Hispanics endure is the fragmentation within their own community and the fragmentation between different social groups within the larger society. These divisions make even worse the dehumanizing forms of economic and political inequality between groups and within a given group. Group and community life, which is part of the traditional and enduring identity of most Hispanics, does not entail a disregard for individuality and individual choices. It does, however, represent one dimension of our resistance to the way our present culture devalues group life and the role group life has in empowering individuals and making them whole.

The notion of justice that stresses power and community as central values also entails other values that are central to the Hispanic moral point of view, in particular the values of freedom, equality, and order. In this perspective, freedom entails more than what is normally understood by the term "human rights." It entails being safe from undue intervention (freedom *from*), but it mainly implies accountability, obligations, and responsibilities to others (freedom *for*). Given the reality of domination and exploitation experienced by most Hispanics, to become truly free one must serve *the other*, in particular the poor and powerless within society. Freedom is not limited to the formal dimension of choice making, but it is related to the more classical sense of choosing what is right and what promotes the well-being of the community. It is to serve the community with compassion and love, and at times even to sacrifice one's own interest for the well-being of the whole.

Equality is defined in comparative terms. It consists of the actualization of the relative well-being of all social groups and the social commitment to overcome those forms of socioeconomic inequality that make it difficult for people to *recognize* and relate to one another as equals. As a minimum, economic inequalities cannot exceed a reasonable limit.

When power serves justice, and justice sustains freedom and equality as defined here, it is reasonable to expect that order will emerge and sustain itself. Politically speaking, order is an important moral value. It provides the much-needed network of regularity and predictability that enables us to rely on, depend on, and trust one another. However, order is not foundational to but *derivative* of the values of power, freedom, equality, and community. It is the consequence of the capacity different social groups have for acting with relative autonomy, free from the undue intervention of other groups, of having the resources they need to survive and flourish as a group and as individuals, and of providing public spaces for different groups to gather to negotiate a life in common without surrendering what is essential to their being.

CIVIL SOCIETY AS THE LOCUS OF JUSTICE

Hispanics also struggle for the emancipation of their communities within the social sphere.[7] In this view, the language of domination and exploitation points to the absence of strong social institutions whose function it is to serve and protect Hispanic interests. The emancipation of our community depends on its capacity to create a plethora of economic and social services whose purpose it is to assist and direct

Hispanics in our quest toward a better state of affairs. The creation of a network of strong institutions is necessary if we are to advance our self-realization and autonomy. Social institutions provide centers of authority by which the community can organize, in light of its values and traditions, its internal life. They also enable us to relate to and influence the dominant society. If we are victimized by distorted stereotypes, we need to promote our own positive self-image by creating our own magazines, radio stations, movies, and TV programs. These will provide our community and society at large with an alternative and more accurate vision of who we are, what our culture is, and what we value. A strong institutional base will allow us to make other institutions more responsive to our needs, particularly when we are not able to develop them by ourselves.

Institutions play a prominent role in determining the practices that shape our communal and individual behavior. They are part of that network of social relationships that plays a significant role in molding our collective and individual character. Social activists have a preference for character ethics just as political activists have a preference for the ethics of principle. One of the virtues of our liberal democratic society is that it allows for the establishment of independent institutions and voluntary associations that provide alternative social spaces where we can live in light of the values we hold dear, and which are relatively free from government control and the coercive presence of the state.[8] Efforts to create autochthonous institutions are worthy of our support since they preserve and nourish our beloved traditions. Such institutions are worthy of our respect since they enable us to pursue, *in an orderly manner,* new ways of transforming our practices and of expressing our identity.

Dignity in this perspective has an institutional base. It has to do with, among other things, our disciplined and faithful commitment to sustaining those institutional practices by which the needs of our people are served and cared for. Dignity is expressed through the various ways in which individuals and communities become self-reliant and thus responsible agents in determining their individual and collective future. And dignity is related to our becoming less dependent on the state and more self-disciplined and directed.

85

In the perspective of social activists, the formation of upright moral character is at the center of our emancipation. What the poor need more than anything else, is the power to become a different kind of person. A stronger sense of personal moral responsibility, a spirit of self-reliance, and a sense of spiritual renewal are all essential parts of the process to emancipate the poor. If the poor correct those character flaws that affect day-to-day relations with their loved ones and their more intimate communities, their condition will improve and so will the condition of the larger Hispanic community. Structural change as advocated by the political activists may be necessary, but it is not primary. To significantly change our moral character must remain our focus and our primary concern.

For those who struggle for justice within the social sphere, the accusation made by the political activists, that all present social institutions are oppressive and cannot be counted on to help the community achieve its emancipation, is misplaced and uninformed. Such accusations and their overall negative attitudes and suspicion toward institutions merely express a cynical and naive understanding of the value of institutions, and an equally naive belief that Hispanics can effect social change only through the political process. The social activists argue that Hispanics are too few in numbers, too diverse in their ethnic and national loyalty, and geographically too dispersed to build the kind of coalitions needed to make a significant political difference. Our political capacities and experiences are presently too weak, and the power against us too strong, for us to center all our hopes for emancipation in the political arena. Furthermore, Hispanics demonstrate a political preference for issues that affect the local community, and are somewhat indifferent about national politics.[9] In short, those who advocate and rely solely on direct political intervention will ultimately prove it to be a less effective vehicle of change than the institutional approach.

Hispanic churches are identified by social activists as key institutions in the movement toward emancipation. The political activist, given the basic antipolitical attitudes of most Hispanic churches, would not point to the church as a center of political empowerment. Pentecostal and free churches in particular, have a greater capacity to congregate larger sectors of the Hispanic community than any other institution within the community, and to mobilize them with enthusiasm and faithfulness.[10] Churches also enjoy a privileged position of trust within and outside the Hispanic community. They are perceived as institutions that care and contribute to strengthening the institution of the family (which many Hispanics still identify as the basic social institution), and that can remedy some of the social evils which infect the Hispanic community, such as addictions to drugs, alcohol, and gambling. The church is also in the privileged position of being able to offer the community a number of critically needed services such as child care, care for the elderly, alternative schools, organized sports activities, and other communal programs that the state has tended to ignore.[11] Because we receive from the church care and recognition, the ethics that fits our cultural sensibilities, Hispanics give it authority in our life.

Social activists, unlike their political counterparts, view society as being relatively open to change and improvement—and as essentially harmonious and ordered. This is the foundation of their hopeful attitudes. Their reformist and gradualist attitude is based on the conviction that most Hispanic institutions are, by and large, faithful servants of the community. They embody the values and goals that fit our way of life and are a positive presence for the well-being of the community. This makes them legitimate centers of authority, and explains why most members of society, including the poor, support them. They are reformist and gradualist also because they are convinced that, in spite of the real discrimination and exploitation Hispanics are subjected to, the institutions of our society are healthy and can be made more responsive to our needs. Nonetheless, they do not disregard the need for countervailing power. They encourage local constituencies to remain vigilant and push for reforms whenever institutions do not follow their internal procedures, when they fail to represent authentically their constituency, or when they betray their intended purpose and goals.

Political activists accuse social activists of being overtrustful of the openness of the social order and of its capacity to make room for us. They also claim that social activists are overnostalgic about our culture and limit their definition of culture to folklore. In their view, social activists are advocates of middle-class values and are oblivious to the uniqueness and significantly different social conditions that Hispanics, particularly third- and fourth-generation poor Hispanics, confront in the United States. And they do not recognize the limits and the damaging effects that assimilation will have for Hispanics. Social activists point out that the political activists, in their zeal for change, underestimate the centrality and need for *order* in social life. Also, their conflictual understanding of society and their focus on society as a whole, rather than on local communal issues, is oblivious to the threat of anarchy and chaos that already afflicts and undermines the well-being of the Hispanic community. In their view, it is a gross tactical mistake to assume that the community can risk a greater level of conflict and chaos to pursue the promise of some greater future harmony, reconciliation, and solidarity. Our communities are already infected with too much chaos and lack of order, which negatively affect family life, the workplace, and other spheres of social existence. More than anything else, our communities need principles and institutions to order, regulate, and give direction to our life. Politics, therefore, ought not to be obsessed with change, but ought also to promote and preserve social order.

These disagreements between Hispanics who struggle within the political and social spheres are neither arbitrary nor a matter of temperament. They are based on differing convictions of how the world works and how values are related to one another. They are grounded in our convictions and beliefs of how malleable our social world is and how fast we can change it. From the perspective of the social sphere, individuals are the main subject of change. People change gradually and slowly and need the assistance of institutions to be able to alter their behavior. From the political perspective, the social structure is the main subject of change, and we are not only able to push harder and faster for that change, but not to do so could perpetuate our condition of powerlessness.[12]

Regarding the issue of power, those who work within the social sphere agree that power is necessary for the community to be able to defend and assert its interests. However, in their view, power should be widely distributed so that more institutions can realize their goals. Whenever one sector of society is able to accumulate too much power, weaker institutions and the interests they represent will be threatened. At present, it is preferable for Hispanics, who have only weak institutions, to advocate an even wider distribution of power, which will give them more autonomy and more ability to compete with other centers of power. From this perspective, the emphasis on the accumulation of power upheld by the political activists will most probably be manipulated ideologically by those who already wield power in order to justify and expand the inordinate power they have.

For social activists, power is not ruled by the dynamics of a zero-sum game, nor are social values the outcome of the fragile consensus of unstable and temporary power plays. Social institutions are capable of providing different social groups with the power, stability, and recognition they need to be able to negotiate a common life together. Because institutions provide their constituency with power and recognition, politics can take place on the basis of persuasion and argumentation, rather than by coercion and manipulation. Power remains necessary, but must be properly channeled and contained through socially accepted procedures that allow citizens to express and pursue their interests in an orderly and civil manner.

From the perspective of the social sphere, *order*, as a moral value, is neither derivative nor secondary. On the contrary, social order is foundational for the good life and for the possibility of a community living in light of its self-given moral values. Religiously speaking, power is grounded in God's creative capacity to initiate new beginnings, and institutional order is an expression of that ontological ordering through which God sustains communal life and keeps it human. Institutions and the order they provide *free us from* chaos and the inherent uncertainty and insecurity which chaos and instability bring. Because we live in an ordered and well-structured society we are able to enjoy the *freedom to* pursue new possibilities of life. As such, social institutions and the regularity and order they provide are essential elements in the historical process of any people's humanization.

Therefore, *order* rather than *power* becomes the highest and first principle of social well-being. However, order, like power, is not an end in itself. It is foundational and at the service of the emergence of other moral values, in particular the value of freedom. A well-ordered society enhances freedom. As we just mentioned, negatively speaking, order *frees us from* the instability, uncertainty, and ambiguity of chaos, which is part of anarchy. Positively speaking, order enables us to experience *freedom as an act of self-initiation.* In short, a well-ordered society preserves our freedom by curtailing undue interference from other individuals and institutions, and allows us the liberty to do as we please.

Social activists give freedom a substantive definition different from that given by the political activists. There is a shift in focus from a communal view of freedom, where freedom consists of service to others and acts of sacrifice to promote the well-being of the whole, to a more narrowly defined sense of freedom as liberty or license. Freedom as liberty, is grounded in well-defined rights that allow individuals to initiate action and be protected from the undue intervention and coercive manipulation of others. This view of freedom has a more individualistic bent to it; the freedom of the individual is what counts, and it is not clear that groups, while enjoying certain rights, are to be made the main agents of social and political activity. Groups are, by and large, secondary to individuals.

Freedom, in this view, does not necessitate the communal controls of power and economic resources. It is more directly related to democratic procedures and representative government, and economically it supports the procedural nature of the free market. Both of these institutions, liberal democracy and the free market, have shown themselves quite adept at securing and enhancing the freedom of the individual to live according to her or his choices. These, and other social institutions derived from them, have the virtue of limiting the capacity of the state to intervene in one's life. It is precisely the quest to protect and increase individual freedom that motivates the social activists' commitment to political and economic structures that promise the widest distribution and division of power within society.

Social activists tend to have a procedural view of justice. Justice no longer consists of the creation of a participatory community that promotes group difference and pursues the relatively equal provision of basic necessities for all social groups within. Rather, justice consists of the creation of institutional procedures which guarantee individuals an equal opportunity to compete for the social positions, goods, and services available within society. It consists of the establishment of social procedures that sustain and promote the freedom of all members of society. Equality of opportunity may or may not entail the provision of basic goods and services. That is, equality of opportunity can be either *fair,* where assistance is provided for the less fortunate members of society, or *formal,* where the opportunity to compete and be included is what matters.

Social activists recognize that freedom as liberty feeds social inequality. However, in their view, as long as the institutional procedures are fair, people abide by them, and no one is coerced or cheated, the inequalities that result from our free and voluntary transactions are fair and just. In this view, Hispanics are socially disadvantaged, mostly because we have been deprived of the opportunity and incentive to participate in the process where people compete for those privileged social positions available in society. Social activists claim that justice must focus on the question of equal opportunity, not results. This is one of the areas of discord between the social and political sphere alternatives. The latter claims that the existence of significant economic and social discrepancies between social groups is itself a sign that there has not been equality of opportunity, and that results must remain a legitimate concern of justice. Political activists claim affirmative action programs are needed to include us in the economic and political spheres, while social activists claim these programs limit our participation and distort our achievements.

Social activists argue that to deal with the question of massive poverty and economic inequality, it is important that Hispanics create self-help institutions and try to rely less on the political state. State welfare agencies are seen as contributing to and perpetuating the poverty and lack of self-worth that affects Hispanics in disproportionate ways, and as generating dependency and a sense of impotence. Again, institutions such as the church and other charity organizations have to be organized to attend to the needs of the poor. Finally, social activists uphold a contractual as opposed to an organic notion of social groups and community. Communities, like institutions, are the result of voluntary transactions. We create and support them because we expect to derive at least as much benefit from them as the investment we place in them. Communal life is not intrinsic to what it means to be human, it is rather an instrumental good; it provides the goods and services we need to enjoy the good life. Community exists for the sake of individual freedom. This point of view is also individualistic. There is nothing more dangerous or detrimental to social life within the

United States, say the social activists, than to abandon our commitment to individual rights and freedom for the sake of group life. Group identification can lead only to the victimization of the individual. The political activists agree that communities are to a great extent contractual, but they view social groups as organic. They are intrinsically intertwined with our personal identity and as such are owed specific loyalty and care on our part. Social activists have faith that the values of the liberal tradition will eventually enable Hispanics to achieve their full emancipation, mainly through the process of social integration.

CULTURE AS THE LOCUS OF JUSTICE

Hispanics also struggle for the emancipation of our people within the sphere of culture. The cultural activists agree with the political and social activists that power and order are central values in the creation of a good and just society, but they have a different understanding of the causes and dynamics of our oppression and domination. For them there are other, more fundamental issues than the questions of political powerlessness and institutional bankruptcy. Matters pertaining to our cultural identity and to our sense of self-respect and dignity have priority. Questions such as, Who are we as a people? What is our unique contribution to our common life? and, What gives meaning and value to our being? are at the forefront of our justice struggle.[13]

Beyond poverty, powerlessness, and institutional chaos, oppression entails the institutional and systematic disregard and denigration of our racial makeup, language, capacities, heritage, aesthetic values, customs, and traditional habits. These forms of oppression have also had a devastating effect on our community. They undermine the community's sense of self-worth and self-confidence, making it doubt its values and potentialities. Justice is very much a struggle for human dignity. And dignity, from the perspective of the cultural sphere, is defined in terms of our capacity to live in light of our honorable traditions and cultural wisdom. The greatest indignity is to tell us that our ways are less valuable and meaningful than those of others, and that we have to sacrifice our cultural identity for the sake of social and political stability.

The politics of cultural integration and assimilation is at the center of this point of view, and the ideology of the melting pot is singled out as a leading contributing factor to this form of oppression and domination. Cultural activists move within the dialectic of denouncing cultural imperialism and struggling for cultural affirmation. Culturally speaking, to be oppressed and dominated is to lack the resources and power to secure the continuation of one's group's cultural heritage. It is to be made socially vulnerable and invisible, in which one's social experiences and cultural interpretations are seen as having less or no value than those of dominant groups. It is to have views that never influence the dominant culture and to have to accept the views and values of the dominant group as a way of moving ahead socially. We must keep in mind that Anglos can live and progress without ever encountering or entering the world of Hispanics, but we cannot improve our lot without entering the world of our oppressors and compromising and negotiating with them, mostly on their terms.[14]

Cultural activists believe that the preservation of their Hispanic cultural heritages is a source of strength and empowerment for their comunidad and their individual well-being. Loyalty and commitment to group cultural life is a dominant belief among Hispanics. This belief is foundational to the ethics of care and recognition, which makes the preservation of group identity one of our main moral obligations. We resist surrendering our group commitment to live by the individualistic standards of the dominant culture because we have experienced the vulnerability we place ourselves in when we live at the margins of our group. We also believe that lack of group solidarity will delay our dignified integration into the dominant society.

One element of the Hispanic sense of dignity is the capacity for being authentic to the cultural heritage and traditions that provide us with a sense of meaning and purpose in life. Dignity in this view, is not only a private issue, but very much a reality tied to the existence and enhancement of la comunidad and the cultural traditions by which the people express their sense of self. This is why, whenever our culture is ridiculed or distorted, Hispanics argue that our dignity is being violated. This is at the heart of the issue of the melting pot.

The ideology of the melting pot affirms a three-level process of social integration and assimilation. The first generation barely assimilates itself, keeping the language, lifestyle, and culture of the homeland. The second generation moves between both cultural systems; children are fluent in two languages, know and can manage the idiosyncrasies and nuances of both cultures. The third and subsequent generations experience a significant dilution of their cultural identity and become fully integrated into the new society. Our social institutions, in particular social schools, have as part of their mission to foster the process of cultural dilution and to shape a new identity. Migrants are expected to surrender their culture and adopt a new one: a North American identity defined in terms of one's commitment to liberal democracy and individual rights.[15] All migrants are expected to become some type of Anglo Saxon, sharing common values and beliefs.

Cultural activists point out that Hispanics continue to show resistance to melting! We resist because we value our life in comunidad, our culture and traditions, our religious heritage and practices, all of which bestow our life with meaning and purpose. On the negative side, our continuous and relentless experience of discrimination and social marginality creates skepticism regarding the desire and sincerity of dominant groups to include us. Our struggle for cultural affirmation, however, is not a mere reaction to the entrenched resistance European Americans have toward Hispanics. We hold tenaciously to our ways because we know their rich and abundant resources, and the power that narratives, symbols, and structures of meaning have in enabling us to confront the diverse personal, social, spiritual, and political challenges in our lives.

Cultural activists argue that equal and full membership, the greatest gift one people can give another, will result from our surrendering our cultural particularity. There is something fundamentally wrong and even cruel with the notion that, as a condition of social inclusion, we must surrender the culture that cements our identity. We have come to believe that social acceptance, acceptance with dignity, is never a gift but the outcome of a struggle. We have survived within the United States because of our enduring loyalty to our comunidad and our culture. Group solidarity and loyalty, more than conversion to individualism and abstract notions of democracy and human rights, continue to be for us the basis of what little empowerment we have been able to achieve.

For the cultural activist, given the group makeup of our country, monoculturalism and monolingualism are the only way to secure social unity and stability. It seems more logical to affirm that social unity and stability are enhanced by creating a social structure that makes it impossible for some social groups to dominate others. It is not the plurality of culture and group life that creates instability, but the fact that some groups are powerful and can dominate those who are powerless.

The increased consciousness of the importance of group life and cultural authenticity among Hispanics can be seen on a number of fronts. For example, Hispanic churches that, for the most part, are apolitical or conservative in their political options, are a strong front in the struggle for group affirmation and resistance to cultural imperialism. Through the preservation and celebration of folklore, Spanish, and the provision of a quasi-public space where Hispanics have occasions to organize their community life, they support group differences and resist the drive toward value and cultural sameness. Hispanic congregations more and more become communities of cultural resistance.

Within every mainline denomination, where Hispanics are once again defined and treated as a minority, we seek exceptions to the way the dominant European American brethren do things. We argue, for example, for the need for caucuses, special curricula, liturgical resources, language conferences or presbyteries, to represent our interests and concerns. When these are not provided we feel at ease using the liturgical and educational resources made by other denominations, including resources that do not fit us theologically, but that are culturally fitting. These demands for the denomination to subsidize and guarantee our present and future ecclesiastical existence are nothing more than a call for Anglos to move beyond tolerance and relate to us in terms of recognition and respect.[16] We expect the denomination to help subsidize and guarantee our cultural existence as a unique expression of the one Church of Jesus Christ.

Cultural activists recognize that the social advancement of Hispanics, both as individuals and as culture-bearing groups, depends on our ability to negotiate a common life with the dominant cultural group. There are levels of assimilation and acculturation that will inevitably take place, and which our children cannot escape. Our children live their lives as North American citizens, and it is normal for them to seek to be full citizens and to define their identity accordingly. They will find some of the symbols, narratives, and values of the dominant Anglo Saxon culture more adequate for dealing with the challenges and quest for meaning in their lives. It is to be expected that as a people who dwell within two cultural systems, one at home and one dominant in the public spaces of society, we devise a new identity that manifests various forms of double consciousness.[17] What cultural activists do not accept is the stereotypical way our culture is portrayed. This portrayal promotes among our youth, but not exclusively among them, an attitude of shame, self-denial, and self-loathing, and among European Americans fear and aversion, which lead to practices of discrimination against us.

Cultural activists continue to argue that, while the melting pot has worked fairly well for most European immigrants, it has proved to be quite detrimental to people of African and Latin American descent. Part of the problem is that we, unlike the Europeans, are not really immigrants. Migrants chose to abandon their nation and to assume the language, history, and culture of their newly adopted nation. African Americans came as slaves, Mexican Americans were forcibly annexed to the nation, Puerto Ricans became a war bounty of the war between Spain and the United States, and Native Americans were the original inhabitants of the land. In a somewhat literal sense, we did not come to the nation, the nation came to us. And many of us share a consciousness and history of being not just another migrant group, but of being members of conquered and colonized nations and peoples. As we were incorporated into the nation, it was never our intention to abandon our language and culture. This has been the intention of the dominant group, one we have resisted to the best of our abilities and against insurmountable odds. From our point of view the United States is a federation of nations, not just a plurality of ethnic groups. And as such it makes sense for us to demand special rights and privileges to ensure the survival of our national and cultural heritage.

The ideology of the melting pot did not have us in mind, nor has it ever included us in its vision and understanding of *the melt*. Racial and ethnic groups were and remain victims of that racism that constitutes the main sickness, and the most obvious contradiction and failure, of the founding ideals of the United States of America. While individual members of our racial and ethnic group are accepted and even melted, we as a group are still rejected. It is important to understand that rejection is a group phenomenon. Even today, if we are fortunate enough to have achieved some level of political and economic success—and individual members of these ethnic groups have become prominent figures within the nation—as a racial and ethnic group we remain second- and third-class citizens. In the best of cases, the insistence that only one culture be normative and dominant cannot but humiliate those asked to abandon their cultural heritage in order to adapt to that culture which defines them as being less..

Cultural activists denounce the unidirectional and one-dimensional process of social integration imposed upon us as being an affront to our dignity. Racial and ethnic minorities, while forced to exist as outsiders, are still expected to take responsibility for integrating themselves into the dominant society. We are the ones called to abandon our cultural heritage and assimilate into Anglo Saxon culture. However, Anglos do not have to work toward integration; they have nothing to give up or adapt to. Cultural activists are not opposed to integration; they advocate for a real multicultural encounter among the plurality of social groups, each one taking responsibility to understand the idiosyncrasies of the others and actually recognize, respect, and learn from the others.

Our sense of group identity was heightened during the struggles for civil rights. We owe African Americans a great debt for our recommitment to the quest for our cultural roots. However, dimensions and elements of the civil rights struggle have made it more difficult for Hispanics to affirm our legitimate demands for national and cultural rights. The civil rights movement has been a struggle for social justice, seeking color blind laws to replace the institutionalization of "separate but equal treatment." Segregated schools, in particular, were found and denounced by the courts as perpetuating a "badge of inferiority" among African Americans. The struggle against racial discrimination led to an understanding of injustice as the condition of being arbitrarily excluded from dominant social institutions. And we came to understand justice as nondiscrimination and being allowed equal opportunity to participate in the benefits provided by our dominant institutions. This understanding of justice has left the impression that any kind of preferential treatment on the basis of national or cultural origin is essentially discriminatory, and in substance no different from the former laws of segregation. But from the perspective of cultural activists, this misunderstands the limits and the spirit of the laws against desegregation.

What civil rights activists challenged, and with what the courts agreed, was that the claim made by segregationists that African American children were in fact obtaining the same education as white children, was simply not the case. Segregationists did not claim that African Americans were a different nation, or that they were entitled to an education based on different language and cultural presuppositions. Segregationists claimed that the facilities, in spite of economic and structural disparities, were, educationally speaking, equally adequate. Their claim was that the communities were racially segregated but the education was the same. African Americans complained that they were being forcibly excluded from the main institutions of society and that this was damaging to their self-image and to the real advancement of their people. This was the point that was challenged in the Supreme Court.

From the Hispanic point of view, this aspect of the civil rights struggle does not address the key issues of the national integrity and rights of racial and ethnic minorities. The rights we pursue are those needed by culturally distinct groups, that is, the rights of peoples and nations that the court decision against segregation did not address. The arguments for racial integration neither support nor negate our claims for autonomous institutions, special types of political representation, or other types of preferential treatment such as multilanguage education, which we need in order to preserve our distinct cultural heritage and to ensure our future existence. Our complaint, similar to that presented by Native Americans, is that we are forcibly included or integrated into a culture and way of life that is not our own, and that our own is not given its due recognition.

The state, in the name of neutrality, actually enforced upon us the dominant language of the nation and its Anglo Saxon system of values. And it is this forced integration which represents for us a "badge of social inferiority" and an undignified way of life. From the perspective of the cultural activist, the same principle should apply for both African

American and Hispanic American people, that is, racial classifications that are harmful ought to be prohibited. Racism for African Americans comes from denying them full membership within the community. Racism for Hispanics comes from denying that we are a culturally distinct people with our own cultures and communities.

If the notion of cultural rights or national autonomy within the larger political culture is not required by liberalism, it is not in principle inconsistent with it. Liberals are correct in pointing out that such recognition does entail social and political tensions. Cultural activists respond that these social and political tensions can be solved through negotiation. It is imperative, however, that we recognize that well-defined national cultural groups are entitled to special group treatment and that this does not entail that all social groups are entitled to the same. Those of us who were incorporated into the nation should not be treated the same way as those who chose to come and integrate themselves. Our claim for special group life in no way violates the rights of immigrants. And we will continue to resist being treated unjustly for the sake of the dominant group's needs for and feeling of security and stability. Cultural activists point to the fact that our society is already multicultural and multilingual. It makes no sense for a nation which cannot escape being at the vanguard of the new world order to force monoculturalism and monolingualism on its citizens. Such a backward move reveals lack of creative imagination, a mean-spirited nativism, and an inclination to be tribal. Many Hispanics consider these attitudes and demands not only an affront to our dignity but also a threat to our survival and well-being.

For the cultural activist, if Hispanics abandon our cultural heritage we risk becoming bereft of a communal context whose symbols, rituals, and narratives allow us to derive a positive sense of meaning and direction for our lives.[18] If we betray our ethnic loyalties, we will remain politically weak and socially marginal—socially invisible people who must endure the threatening experience of being nonpersons in an alien land. Many Hispanics today painfully experience and know invisibility.

Cultural activists envision a just society in which diverse social groups are allowed to maintain their differences and are empowered to negotiate a common life together. Integration does not assume value commonness, but a common commitment to providing the goods and services for the different social groups to survive and the spaces they need to come to know one another. Social stability is secured through the relative equal empowerment of the various social groups. And the new social order, while treating nationally defined social groups differently, will still sustain a system of rights that is common to all groups. The rights in question seek to protect *all* groups from the tyranny of the majority or dominant groups.

In a just society, each social group is able to reclaim its cultural roots and traditions. Among other things, this entails the retrieval of ancestral history, or those indigenous beginnings which embody the wisdom of the people. The crises that have shaped the character of the people are retold, and important events and achievements are brought to light. Heroes are rediscovered and the people are made aware of their contributions to the arts—music, painting, poetry, literature—and to the sciences. Most important, the people retrieve the history of their political and social struggles, which embodies the memory of resistance and survival that is central to their character. Genuine history, however, is not for the sake of therapy and personal or group well-being. As such, it must narrate the stories of abuses and those shortcomings of the community which also shape its identity. The less glamorous dimension of our history can encourage us to be more tolerant of the shortcomings of other social groups and, in solidarity with them, try to enhance justice for all members of society. As Justo González points out, "Once we are agreed that we are all *ladrones*, it will be easier for all of us to see more clearly into issues of justice."[19]

But it is not enough to rediscover the history of how and why Hispanics came to be in America or to reaffirm their traditional cultural heritage. It is equally important that Hispanics, particularly the latter generations, find the space and support they need to give expression to their new identity as Hispanic Americans. It is interesting to notice how first- and second-generation Hispanic churches struggle with these issues. These churches, usually dominated by the older generation, expend great effort preserving the culture and ways of the homeland for the young. Usually they worship in their own language and celebrate traditional festivals and folkloric events. Still, by and large, these churches do not do an adequate job of enabling the young, particularly the third and fourth generations, to express their own identity as Hispanics who no longer just live in the United States, but who are Hispanic Americans with no knowledge of a culture or home other than the one provided by this society. This has led to fragmentation and to the growth of internal conflicts within many church communities and within the Hispanic community at large. In the absence of autonomous institutions that preserve our cultural identity, it makes sense that many of our young choose to assimilate. But even if there were such autonomous institutions, it is still their right to assimilate if they choose to do so.

The dynamics of social integration and cultural authenticity encourage cultural activists to pay particular attention to educational or school politics. One issue on which Hispanics come to work together is in the struggle to keep bilingual education and the teaching of Spanish within our public schools. Cultural activists, as well as many political and social activists, deal with the politics of language at two levels: as a matter of cultural identity and in terms of the ways language is used as a tool for domination and exploitation. Let us deal with the second issue first.

Cultural activists point out that language serves to veil those negative beliefs and attitudes that lead to oppressive social practices. That is, the use of politically correct language does not entail that true feelings and beliefs are made public. Not all who publicly affirm our equality of worth and dignity are free from the fears and aversions of those identified as other or deviant. These fears and aversions are hidden, but they remain alive and remain quite damaging. As a people we are feared because we are poor and forced to live the culture of poverty, because we are racially mixed, which for some is more offensive than being black, and because we are culturally different and resist becoming monolingual. Those who fear us proclaim publicly that we are their equals, but they disclose their fear and prejudices through the gestures, tone of voice, glances, attitudes, and body language that structure the everyday encounters between our two cultures, cementing the structural domination in which we live.

Cultural activists continue to argue that many of us have become so accustomed to these discriminatory practices that we treat them as if they were natural. But they are not. They are cultural, political, and social constructions whose significance becomes clear in the way they affect all decisions having to do with who will work, obtain loans, be promoted, and who is recognized as having authority. Demeaning stereotypes, habits, and comportment can and must be subjected to our political consideration and collective choices. They fall within the purview of justice, since it is the social structure that makes these dehumanizing practices possible and acceptable.

Cultural activists seek to politicize these oppressive habits and demeanors. They want to make them the object of public debate and discussion as a way to enhance cultural awareness among the population at large and to forward the values of living within a pluralistic, multicultural social context. Public debate, exposure, and dialogue between the different cultural groups will enhance our awareness that we are able to change those habits, gestures, and practices that are harmful. By creating public spaces for cross-cultural encounters and conversations, we may be able to discover that cultural diversity, when all social groups are empowered, far from being a threat to national unity and stability, can lead to the creation of a more inclusive and thus humane and stable social order.

The creation of public spaces that provide occasions to discuss our group differences can lead to a more comprehensive understanding of why we consider Spanish and bilingual education important not only for Hispanics, but also for the larger political community. Supporters of the English-only movement do so on economic, political, and social grounds. It is a matter of saving tax money by eliminating services provided to Spanish speakers, such as voting instructions and ballots, public signs, bilingual education, and other related services. Others claim that monolingualism supports value commonness and helps preserve and promote social stability. The proliferation of languages and cultural loyalties contributes to fragmenting the Republic, a tendency for which Canada and Central European nations are evidence. Others argue that it is mere common sense that the only way to advance in our nation is for individuals and social groups to master the English language. Otherwise we will remain economically, socially, and politically handicapped and our life prospects will be seriously limited.

Though all of this is true, cultural activists point out that there were Spanish-speaking communities within our borders long before the

British organized their settlements, and that the United States has forced people in Spanish-speaking nations, such as Puerto Rico, to become citizens with Spanish as their dominant language and means of cultural expression. Furthermore, current migration policies will result in more migrants from Latin and Central America and to the preponderance of Spanish as the dominant means of expression and communication within many Hispanic communities. Many Hispanic Americans keep relatively close ties with friends and families in their nation of origin. For many of us, to keep speaking Spanish is a way of preserving and perpetuating family unity. We not only travel back and forth to visit family and friends, but given world trends toward more unity and exposure of different peoples and cultures to one another, the media keeps us informed of what is happening in our former country. Given all these factors, it does not make sense to believe that monolingualism will contribute to national unity and stability. On the contrary, the English-only movement will probably fuel social division and enhance the suspicions and lack of trust between various social and ethnic groups and our main social and political institutions.

Cultural activists do not deny that within socially pluralistic societies there will be tension among the different social groups, just as there are tensions among segments of any given social group. But we insist that it is not the existence of group differences or cultural or language pluralism that is the problem. The problems reside in the structure of domination and oppression that allows one of the groups to exercise dominance over others. Group domination is what generates social instability and disintegration. In our context, the push for social homogeneity and value commonness forces us and other racial and ethnic groups into the position of undignified assimilation and, thus, to postures of resistance whose final result cannot but exacerbate the possibilities of social conflict.

What we need is not to be forced into monolingualism, but to be provided resources to learn and be competent in English as well as in Spanish. Cultural activists point out that bilingual education, as it presently exists, is a misnomer. It does not enhance our language skills but merely enables our children to learn math, science, and other academic subject matter as they continue to master English. Hispanics want to learn English, but we claim that this is not a reason not to keep our own language. What we want is a national commitment to bilingual and bicultural education that both assimilates our children into the mainline and allows them to grow in their culture of origin. Spanish, for us, is more than a tool of communication, it is central to our identity. To let it go for the sake of social acceptance and advancement, which are quite uncertain, is to contribute to the process of self-annihilation and of diminishing our dignity.

Cultural activists recognize that language does not exhaust our whole identity. Many of us do not speak Spanish and are still proud of our Hispanicity. When we put down and make fun of those who do not master our language, we merely reveal that we ourselves are not beyond the dynamics of group oppression and domination.[20] We have to allow individuals and subgroups within the Hispanic community to make choices that are hard for us to understand. We, too, must practice respect for inner group differences, that is, respect for differences within our own racial and ethnic family.

Cultural activists understand better than those who work from within the other two spheres that the debate about schools and the school curriculum is a significant political matter. Public schools ought to become one of the main forums for our children, our future citizens, to learn about the contributions and achievements of each other's racial and ethnic groups. Schools play a prominent role in molding the perceptions and attitudes of future citizens. By gathering children from different cultural backgrounds, ethnic groups, and religious heritages, they will recognize and respect differences among their peers. This is important, if *all* students are to develop a sense of personal self-worth and nourish their sense of dignity and the worth and dignity of others. And insofar as schools do shape the kind of citizens we will have, in order to promote our democratic traditions it is important that schools be well integrated, and that within their walls there be members of the various racial and ethnic groups. School curricula ought to be culturally diverse and sensitive to those who attend school.

The importance of integrated schools is grounded in the fact that, within the school walls, teachers are not the only ones who teach. Students also teach and learn from one another. They teach and learn from one another the art of living together within a culturally pluralistic context and, it is to be hoped, a context of mutual respect and support. Neighborhoods and schools ought to be integrated, because within a democratic and pluralistic society, schools are not just centers where students come to learn how to read and write, but one of the public spaces where they learn how to become citizens capable of living together within a culturally pluralistic and democratic society constituted by social groups different from their own. For schools to be representative of the diversity of our communities, it is necessary that neighborhoods themselves be integrated, which sadly enough is not the case in most communities within the United States.

Cultural activists share values similar to the ones upheld by the social and political activists. They, too, uplift the value of equality. They emphasize the centrality of equal worth and self-respect that comes from being recognized as full members of society. But their understanding of equality is somewhat different from that of the social activist and more diffused than that of the political activist. We need more than mere formal equality of opportunity; we need fair equality of opportunity. Fair equality of opportunity necessitates that, as a matter of social policy, society make an adequate investment of its resources to redress the history of injustice under which most Hispanics have been forced to live. The aim of this social investment is to enable racial and ethnic minorities to compete on a level playing field with their fellow citizens. Job programs and quality education are seen as keys to overcoming the social barriers that have been placed in the way of racial and ethnic minorities. Job training programs and adequate employment are particularly important factors for generating the kind of social and economic stability that enables the community to sustain itself and prosper.[21]

This notion of social justice focuses on the group rather than on the individual. This priority given to group life is intrinsic to Hispanic culture and our sense of identity. The condition of the ethnic group becomes the standard by which relative well-being is measured and compared. A just society is egalitarian. It seeks not to provide all with the same but rather to keep the inevitable inequalities that are part of social life within reasonable and acceptable limits. Significant inequalities between social groups makes it harder for the weakest parties to assert their right to be recognized and easier for the stronger parties to disregard and override the interests and legitimate claims of the weak.

Regarding the configuration of values, their meaning and way they relate to one another, the cultural activists argue that freedom is more than liberty or the right to do as one pleases, and entails more than merely serving the community. Freedom is understood as the capacity to establish meaningful relationships with others. Mutuality, not self-sacrifice for the sake of the whole, is at the center of this notion of freedom. Freedom and equality are intrinsically related. Only when there is relative equality do people recognize one another as equals and worthy of respect. And only when one has the resources to make meaningful choices can one properly claim to be free. Equality is foundational for power, for an ethnic group to order its internal life, and for relating to others from a position of relatively equal strength. Dignity comes from the dynamics of mutual recognition and mutual support. We are made aware of dignity when we experience the care others express for us, and when they know they can count on our care.

On the negative side, cultural activists make group identity and interests so dominant that it becomes difficult to understand how the group and individuals within it relate to society as a whole. It gives the appearance of being separatist and of fueling social division and social conflict.[22] While they uphold an organic interpretation of the racial and ethnic group, which they see as intrinsically valuable, they understand society in instrumental and contractual terms. And the relationship between racial and ethnic groups and the larger community is also interpreted in contractual and instrumental terms. Society is not necessarily good in itself, but merely provides different groups with the goods and services they need to follow their self-interests and notions of the good life. Within it, different social groups negotiate the conditions under which they will work together. The aim of the larger community becomes fairness and efficiency for the sake of the overall well-being of its racial and ethnic constituencies.

From Value Conflicts to Justice as Solidarity

VALUE CONFLICTS

The different struggles of emancipation we have examined share, at least formally, similar value commitments. They all affirm the values of freedom, equality, power, community, order, and justice as essential to what it means to be human, and to create and live in a good community. This formal agreement should not surprise us. It merely expresses the fact that these are the culturally ingrained moral values that are foundational to our shared political and religious tradition. These struggles for emancipation also share the understanding that moral actions, character development, and caring relationships are not ruled by one value, but by a configuration of values. The moral life is lived in a context of creative tensions between various value commitments.

However, each of these struggles for emancipation organizes the moral principles under a different structure of priority. Political activists give priority to the quest for power, making it foundational for creating and sustaining community. Power, in this position, is at the service of securing each social group the recognition and equality it needs to flourish and nurture itself. Power is foundational for mutual recognition and respect. A society of relatively equally empowered social groups will impose limits on the degree of inequality that will be tolerated. And when groups and individuals are empowered and equally recognized, they will be able to exercise their freedom. Freedom will not be mere license, but will be exercised through acts that support structures of mutual accountability and that contribute to and serve the community. Community, in this view, is an intrinsic part of one's self-realization. Order emerges and sustains itself as the natural outcome of groups being empowered in a relatively equal manner, and being equally recognized and respected.

Social activists argue that social order is the first good that has to be secured. Where there is order, individuals can, in the absence of external constraints, exercise their freedom and pursue those individual and communal goals that give content to their life plan. Justice is done when freedom is promoted. And since freedom and equality are

107

conflicting social values, insofar as freedom always generates inequality, society should secure equality of opportunity but never seek equality of results. Community is seen as the result of an agreement between free and autonomous individuals who seek to promote their freedom.

Cultural activists start with a substantive notion of equality. All culture-bearing groups are in principle equal, and the community must provide them with what they need to ensure that future generations will carry on their traditions. They are also committed to the notion that society must not only prevent the gap between the rich and the poor from growing wider, but must attempt to narrow the gap and bring the different social groups to greater relative equality. Equality sustains the empowerment of social groups and creates favorable conditions for community. As the political activists argue, justice is the structuring of the value of freedom and equality where equality is seen as the foundation for freedom. There is a conflict between freedom and equality, but it is not antagonistic, and thus, in enhancing equality we do not undermine freedom in any morally significant way.

The different ordering given by each alternative to the system of values is ultimately a matter of political prudence, that is, of the way each position understands how, in the real world, values relate, follow, and depend on one another. Although all three positions agree that the values of freedom, equality, and community are essential for what it means to be human and for the possibility of creating and sustaining a just society, they each give these terms substantially different, and at times antagonistic, meanings. Although they all use the same terms to describe their value commitments, when we look carefully at what they signify, we can see that they actually uphold significantly different value commitments. This accounts for differences in visions of the good and just society, and for the potential antagonism among different sectors of the Hispanic community, which gets in the way of working in common for justice.

And as long as freedom is narrowly understood as liberty or license, that is, wanting to do as one pleases and being left alone to do so (as defined by social activists), and equality is understood as entailing sameness (a view common among cultural activists), and the creation and maintenance of community loyalty is seen as implying and justifying a high level of personal self-sacrifice from individual members (as political activists seem to imply), then the principles will, in fact, be antagonistic toward one another and each Hispanic group and subgroup will be at odds or, at best, be working parallel to one another. The philosophical and moral differences among these struggles of emancipation, then, are real, but what may be more significant is that these philosophical and moral obstacles could become practical obstacles for Hispanics coming to work together in the struggle to emancipate their people.

THE STRUGGLE FOR JUSTICE AND THE POSSIBILITIES OF HISPANIC SOLIDARITY

In light of our foregoing analysis, we can affirm that for most Hispanics the fundamental problems confronted by our community are those of too much dehumanizing poverty, equally dehumanizing powerlessness, and too little self-respect and self-love, accompanied by a disproportionate sense of self-loathing. We are conscious of the complexity and multilevel nature of the oppression and domination to which our people are subjected. We know that the problems we confront are too complex and urgent to be dealt with effectively within only one of these spheres or by one sector of our community.

The different spheres are related to and condition one another. Still, the problems and challenges we confront within each of them must be dealt with on their own terms. It is possible, for example, as witnessed by the Hispanic middle class (although not only by them), to be free from dehumanizing forms of poverty, have meaningful work and even some degree of power, yet still be enslaved by the internalization of the negative images the dominant society projects on us and our culture, which make us prone to reject and feel shame toward our Hispanicity. On the other hand, we can possess a positive image of self and still forget that without political power and economic resources our sense of values and of being can become folkloric, that our values and being can remain abstract ideals with minimal possibility of being incarnated within history.

The divisions and disagreements that exist within the larger Hispanic community are not only rooted in differences in our moral values and political goals, they are equally rooted in the plurality of our national and racial and ethnic identity. We tend to define our identity primarily in terms of national origin. The fact that we stress our quite nuanced cultural differences, we are widely dispersed, overfocused on issues that affect our particular subgroup within the local community, and give minimal attention to what other Hispanics are doing in other places, has not helped us to be in solidarity with one another. This has also made it difficult to build a broader and more inclusive sense of identity as Hispanic Americans.

But there is hope; a new age is at hand. A new phenomenon enables Hispanics to work through these divisions. We are more conscious of the fact that, morally and politically speaking, it is only in common struggles and through acts of solidarity and coalition-building that we will be able to overcome the diverse challenges we confront.[23] The gathering and encounters of various Hispanic national groups within many of our larger cities is precipitating a change in our attitudes toward one another and in the way we view ourselves. This concentration of various Hispanic groups has created conditions for us to find ways of working together to solve the common problems our diverse communities confront. We have discovered that being in solidarity does not entail surrendering the particular cultural way we express ourselves. We can struggle in common and still celebrate our differences. These shared struggles for justice are not merely strategically significant in a political sense, but they enable us to shape a new sense of shared identity among various Hispanic groups.[24]

All these factors provide conditions for us to reinterpret the meaning and political significance of the values of freedom, equality, and community. They provide an occasion for us to redefine and give a more comprehensive meaning to the values we identify as essential for keeping life human, and for sustaining a just and good society. The practical implication of this transfiguration of values is that it enhances the possibilities for establishing coalitions and working in solidarity for the well-being of our communities and for the creation of a more inclusive and compassionate society.[25]

We do not need to limit our interpretation of freedom as consisting of liberty or license. Freedom becomes for us *creative agency*, which includes the human capacity to imagine and bring about new possibilities of expressing oneself and relating to others. It is important that all people have what they need to be creative agents in at least one of the dominant spheres of life; otherwise the realization of their humanity is jeopardized. Creative agents are vigilant, suspicious, and critical, but positively motivated and inclined to pursue the vision or historical project of creating a more inclusive and compassionate community.

Equality is no longer defined as sameness or uniformity of treatment. It is defined as the equal recognition of differences that make one the unique being one is. Equal recognition and respect entail unequal treatment if such treatment is necessary to promote and nourish the goodness of one's being. Equality necessitates the creation of structures of mutual recognition and support, but not the enforcement of value commonness, or integration of the different social groups into some amorphous organic unity. We are equal in the sense of being essentially relational and dialogical creatures. We need others, their words and deeds, to be able to become who we are and through whom we define, live out, and find our dignity. We can only flourish within the context of relational dialogue, under the commitments of mutual care and fidelity. More than obeying principles and building character we are first to be caring toward one another. To be fully human one has to undertake obligations toward others beyond what is due them as a matter of right. We were created as men and women to live in faithful and trustful relationships. Faithfulness and mutual commitment alone can keep life human and make communities just. This is why any relationship that entails domination or exploitation entails a breach of fidelity and a continued threat to our humanity.

Community, the greatest longing of most members of this society, does not have to be understood in contractual terms. We value community because we know that we are not just individuals, or merely relational beings, but members of wholes, of complex cultures and nations. Today, economic and political forces drive us, even in spite of ourselves, toward more inclusive communities. Narrow-minded nationalism and other forms of cultural tribalism, which resist the drive toward inclusiveness, bring forth some of the worst cruelty humans commit against one another. The drive toward community, more than ever before, is a basic component of our humanity. Ultimately we have more things in common with one another than things that separate us. This basic fact is what we express through the language of human rights and is at the root of our being able to live in solidarity with one another. A community which empowers the different groups that constitute it and which facilitates our being able to establish bonds of mutuality and solidarity, is a community which is at the same time multicultural and inclusive, and can best allow us to enjoy both our diversity and common humanity.

In making creative agency the substance of liberty, fidelity in relationship the substance of equality, and a participatory community the substance of power, Hispanics give themselves the opportunity to perceive the essential interrelatedness and interdependence that exist between their different struggles of justice and the core moral values that sustain them.

By transfiguring the value of freedom from liberty into creative agency, Hispanics are able to move away from the narrow concern of self-fulfillment to an understanding of self-realization based on *other-regard, care, and service to others.* Those others who are different from us model for us new possibilities of being human. Every creative process reveals itself as an extension of our relational nature. It also allows us to understand better how every act of creation and every creative agent needs and depends on the *community.* How can we be creative in the absence of the active assistance and in the passive witness of others within our community? A truly creative act makes manifest the many ways it is tied to that unbroken chain of creativity that constitutes the legacy from our ancestors. Creation is no longer imprisoned in individuality and subjectivity, it also has a public presence and reveals accountability and gratitude to the community. And as we have freely received from them, we should freely give to those who will come after us. Creative agency, therefore, expresses what is valuable and meaningful for ourselves as well as what is of value, meaning, and service for others.

Freedom understood as creative agency, provides us with a new and broader understanding of the relationship between the community and the individual. Our communities contribute to the creative process by providing us with material and intellectual resources and with a context of meaning within which our creation makes sense. At the same time, community depends on the creative capacity of its *individual members* for its survival and for its reason for being. No authentic community can reasonably and humanly expect from its members only commitment and sacrifice. Communities must support, contribute to, and nourish the creativity and well-being of their individual members. The just community creates conditions for its members to express what makes them unique and distinct from fellow citizens. Diversity and pluralism become the marks of a healthy community.

Finally, a community of creative agents entails a commitment to equal respect and equal regard for all members. Creative agents seek and respect the judgments of our equals in determining the merits of our creations. Equality within a pluralistic community sustains the creative freedom that overcomes sameness and homogeneity. To be treated as an equal is not to be treated the same as everyone else, but to be supported and allowed to be the creative agents we potentially are. To deny or curtail our creativity is to undermine our humanity. There is nothing more unjust and oppressive than to demand the less talented to equal the performance, productivity, and creativity of the talented, and to demand that the exceptionally talented limit themselves to the social medium. But it is equally unjust to deprive persons of the creativity they are capable of generating and of the good life they are able to live. A just society encourages diversity and finds ways of sustaining it while allowing its members to rejoice in their differences.

Hispanics are realizing how important it is to continue to find ways of creating more public spaces and occasions for coming together to inform one another of their achievements and shortcomings. They are valuing more and more the opportunities to share among themselves and with other social groups the particularities of their culture and the reason for being of their political concern. They also recognize the importance of sharing in their different struggles and the need to be critiqued by other Hispanic groups. These encounters can consolidate and serve as a basis for the creation of structures of solidarity between Hispanics, and eventually between Hispanics and other racial and ethnic minority groups. We can work together even though we have different conceptions of the most pressing issues, and even though we work within different spheres. We can work together even though we have different conceptions of the priority and relationships between the values to which we commit ourselves. We can no longer afford to undermine our struggles on the basis of petty divisions and squabbles!

Pettiness feeds that cynical attitude that leads to the vision that there is nothing we can do to change our local or national standing.

Divisions and disagreements will remain, but Hispanics have the political maturity to negotiate them and find accommodations that will be reasonable to all parties. Ultimately what matters is that the Hispanic community be served in ways that allow it to affirm its freedom, power, and cultural identity. The struggle must necessarily take place on many fronts. Sometimes it expresses itself as a great leap where significant achievements are made. Other times it is less glamorous, merely resisting further losses within the political, cultural, and economic spheres. But all of the struggles are necessary and significant, and we must learn how to be a critical voice while at the same time being a motivating voice in one another's struggles. What we need is not a unified movement, but a movement in which honest conversation, constructive critique, and solidarity can take place. We have already begun the journey toward creating a more compassionate and inclusive society. Our capacity to enhance our particular visions to include all those who struggle within the different spheres will get us there faster.

A Shared Vision of Justice

In light of what we have said, Hispanic justice talk moves beyond the narrow *economic* distributive agenda to include the *political* concerns of empowerment and decision making, the issue of *cultural* affirmation, and matters relating to authority, autonomy, the development of skills, and the need for social recognition, all of which are part of the *social division of labor.*

A just economic order has as its priority to free its members from the dehumanizing effects of poverty, and the pain and suffering this entails. It empowers citizens to work politically for a more just distribution of social benefits and burdens. It is only by being politically empowered that citizens become more than mere consumers. They become true citizens, creative agents actively involved in solving the problems that affect their lives in significant ways. Empowered citizens limit the ways the state treats them and controls their lives. For the state and the economic order not to be experienced as a domineering presence or as an unreciprocated authority, they must be subjected to the democratic control of their members. Questions of economic distribution must be dealt with politically so that all citizens can have a voice in how social production will take place, what goals are pursued, and for whose benefit they are designed. Political empowerment enables those who depend on welfare grants to counterbalance the patronizing and punitive attitudes of welfare agents. They are made active participants in the functioning of this system. This allows all of us to recognize their dignity and for them to preserve their self-respect. Their dependency, which ought to be quite temporary, will not deprive them of their right to self-determination, and even when they are dependent they will have the occasion to be recognized in public settings. In our view, economic justice seeks more to overcome oppression than to obtain a more balanced distribution of social goods. Through justice we seek to *be* more rather than merely to *have* more.

In a just political order, all social groups are empowered to be active participants in the decision-making centers through which we establish the laws, rules, and procedures by which we organize our mutual dealings and determine what sacrifices we are willing to undertake in order to achieve socially desirable goals. A just political order is essentially democratic since democracy is the result and the condition for the existence of a just state of affairs. A truly participatory democracy enables us to think of our needs and interests in relation to the needs and interests of others. It cements attitudes of mutual accountability and mutual aid. It upholds a system of basic rights for all citizens and still allows for the different treatment of different social groups for the sake of mutual empowerment and social inclusion.

A just division of labor is one in which all members of society have a real opportunity to obtain and build a plurality of skills and talents so that they can be active participants in the productive process. It gives producers a voice as to how labor is organized and compensated. The workforce is organized in such a way that no one feels that what they do is for another's benefit and not for their own development. And it creates spaces both within and outside the workplace so that people have occasion for autonomous creative activity within publicly recognized settings. Producers are consulted in matters regarding the work they perform, and have the experience of being both followers and leaders. These are all ways in which most workers are freed from low-paying, low-recognition jobs and the indignity of disrespectful treatment that usually accompanies them. Work that is essentially brutish, repetitive, and boring, but socially necessary, will be highly compensated. And prestigious social positions will be distributed in light of the different conceptions of merit held by the different culture-bearing groups within society. Affirmative Action programs that counterbalance the discriminatory inclinations of decision makers and which seek to be more inclusive rather than exclusive, are necessary and acceptable until all groups have relatively equal representation within decision-making centers.

And finally, a just society will allow different national groups to live in light of the values that give meaning to their lives. It is free from the indignity that comes from being told that one has to be other than what one is in order to become a full member of society; and free from the stereotypical portraits that generate within our youth attitudes of self-denial and self-loathing, and aversion and fear of us among dominant groups. It allows different culture-bearing groups the freedom and autonomy they need to live publicly and privately in light of their cultures. A just society creates spaces and occasions for the different groups to come together to share their differences, and learn how to overcome those gestures, habits, speech patterns, and comportment that undermine the dignity of other groups. This is the way to achieve social stability and to forward understanding and respect among the different social groups.

For many of us, our religious commitments provide the vantage point from which to understand and be critical of our moral commitments. We commit ourselves to justice because it is part of our sense of what God is calling us to do. We abide by the ethics of care and recognition because God recognizes and cares for us. It is our purpose in the next chapter to lift up the theological dimensions that are part of the ethics of care and recognition dominant in the Hispanic community.

CHAPTER 3

THE THEOLOGICAL DIMENSION OF THE ETHICS OF CARE

Introductory Comments

God talk is an essential element of our Hispanic identity. Even the movie *Mi Familia* ("My Family") cannot avoid dealing with the religious dimension that is an intrinsic part of Hispanic culture (it is not by accident that the main actors are called José, María, and Jesús). Jimmy, who does not manifest religious interests, carries a statue of the Virgin on the dash of his car and a rosary on the rearview mirrow. Antonia became a nun, which made the family quite proud. Still it is María who represents the religiosity of her culture. She does the religious work for the whole family. She not only does religious acts, but looks at and relates to her world from a theological point of view. Hers is a theological perspective shaped by Roman Catholicism and the religion of indigenous people. The syncretism of her theological perspective, a matter quite common among Hispanics, allows her to confide in the Virgin, fear the evil spirit of the river that claims the life of her son Chucho, and believe that the women who, like Isabel, die when giving birth have the cosmological responsibility of helping the sun set, so in resting it can come back to sustain life.

Overhear any of our conversations and you will encounter one of the following expressions: *Si Diós quiere, Bendito sea Diós, sea la voluntad de Diós, ave María (purísima), Diós te bendiga, ¡hay Diós mío!* and, of course, *Adiós.*[1] We use these and other similar religiously charged expressions to communicate our hopes, frustrations, despairs, and our faith perspective. For the faithful, these phrases communicate our conviction that we exist in relation to, are dependent on, and must respond to that transcendent God who we claim is our creator and sustainer. It is not surprising, then, that at the root of the ethics of recognition and care lies a theology, that is, an interpretation of God and of God's relationship with our world. María derives courage from her religious convictions; they sustain her hope and her struggles. When she is unjustly deported to Mexico, a relative tells her to accept being separated from her family and to trust in the Virgin. To which she replies, "The Virgin cannot want this for my family." When Chucho is murdered and there is nothing she can do to bring him back, she finds consolation in the conviction that it is not the police but the evil spirit of the river who has come back to claim her son years after she saved him from drowning.

The movie cannot escape the stereotype of presenting all Hispanics as Catholic. There are no Protestant characters; still, the basic religiosity of the people is dealt with well. Ever since Protestantism became a significant religious alternative for Latin Americans and Hispanic Americans, Catholics and Protestants have been suspicious of each other, accusing each other of being heretics, cultural traitors, and political and social anarchists, or antibiblical, pagan, and superstitious. Fortunately, at present there is a creative and growing ecumenism among Hispanic Protestants and Catholics. It is an ecumenism of mutual respect and recognition grounded not on common theological beliefs, but on an inclination toward solidarity in the struggle for the emancipation of our community. This has allowed both communities to unveil a significant sphere for common moral thought and political action.

The Theological Task

Theology is a systematic form of reflection that builds on the many meaningful conversations that take place within the church and the culture at large. Essentially it is a dialogical and communal task.[2] The church, in spite of the many commonalities shared by its members, is quite literally a gathering of strangers. Within it, peoples of different social classes, cultures, races, and nations gather within the church to praise God and discern God's purpose and will. These differences inevitably shade our interpretation of the Scriptures and our understanding of God and God's relation to the world. It is not surprising that Christians hold different and at times dissenting perspectives of what it means to be faithful.

The need for dialogue and community that is intrinsic to the theological task is grounded on the reality that no one person or group can grasp the wholeness of a God who, in revealing Godself, remains transcendent, infinite, and mysterious. We need and depend on one another to discover, within worship, common prayer, common study, and through our many other interactions, dimensions of God's purpose that otherwise would go unseen. Theology is the product of a church that values being catholic, that is, that values acting and thinking in light of the whole. It is germane to the church to create spaces and occasions for all its members to recognize one another and share, in a context of trust, respect, care, and mutual support, their insights regarding God's will for us today. Thus our diversity and catholicity in themselves entail an ethic. It is an ethic tied to our understanding of the loving and caring nature that ought to define life within the community of faith. Dialogue, mutual recognition, and respect provide fitting ways to model what it means to be God's people, and a more adequate context for discerning God's will.

Theology, however, entails more than belief and understanding. It also concerns itself with the practical implication of shaping a people capable of creating and sustaining structures of solidarity and mutuality within the church and society at large. Theology begins within community and ends in attempting to make our various communities more inclusive and loving. The understanding it seeks is related to its intention of enabling us to move from the state of being mere strangers toward becoming mutually accountable to one another. Within the church it is the familial language of brothers and sisters, or the language of intimate relationships like friendships, which is prevalent. This language assumes levels of trust even among people who have never before met. This is why Hispanics view and experience the church as being essentially an extended family. I was once invited to Monterrey, Mexico, to lecture on the topic of family values. During my address to Presbyterian pastors and members of their congregations, I made the mistake of calling those there gathered *compañeros*. They were quite prompt and firm in pointing out to me that within the church the proper term is *hermano* or *hermana* (brother or sister). This was not a mere semantic matter, it was a matter of identity, of membership, and, most important, of trust. As a stranger I needed to show that I was trustworthy by my willingness to be an *hermano*. In fact, the more controversial my comments, the more important that trust factor became for all of us to be able to have a meaningful conversation.

Hispanic theology, as a communal task, humbly recognizes and honors the plurality of persons and movements, both past and present, that influence and shape our views of God and God's relation to the world. However, as we believe that no one can do theology alone, we also believe that no one group of people can do theology for others. This is why we refuse to identify what is dominant, either culturally or theologically, with what is universally valid. True theology will embody insights relevant for all members of the community of faith, but what is relevant cannot be defined, much less discerned in its fullness, by one group. Thus, while we acknowledge that we have learned much from European American theology, we also believe that our theological insights are significant not just for Hispanics, but for the community of faith at large.

Hispanic theology is a very contextual response, informed by Scripture, our ecclesial tradition, the challenges we confront within the world, and the time God has given us to live. What is theologically true and universally relevant is tied to concrete and historically limited events and personalities. It is within the concrete and particular that we might be able to unveil something that is meaningful and significant in a more universal way. But the very particularity and historicity of our theological formulations demand that we continue to correct and revise them as we continue to act and think in ways that attempt to be faithful to God. Theology is a never-ending task.

We recognize that our theology is biased. It is tainted by the religious experience and insights of an underrepresented, exploited, and dominated racial and ethnic group. It is biased toward the conquered (those who were annexed to the nation in spite of their choice not to be), the migrants (who choose to leave and become members of a new people), and the refugees (those made stateless by their own nation). We believe in the God of Scripture who is also biased toward those who are denied what is necessary for life and who live in fear. We believe our bias reveals insights as to how God calls us to relate to strangers, and the obligations to those within and outside our immediate family, culture, and nation. They force us to remember God's expectation that we be hospitable to strangers. Face-to-face encounters with those who suffer or live in fear, whether self-chosen or accidental, force upon us the inevitable ethical questions: What ought we to do? What is God calling us to do as individuals and communities? and more significant, Who is my brother and sister when I, my mother, or my loved one is in need? They are recognized and cared for as the sentient persons they are; their unique stories become an occasion to disclose to us who we are and who our God really is. Finally, what is theologically insightful and true can be recognized as such by people outside the community of faith. The insights of our faith can become relevant to the way our nation creates policies for culture-bearing groups, migrants, and refugees.[3] In this way our theology sees as part of its purpose, to contribute to the creation of a more compassionate and inclusive church and nation.

Our theology, therefore, does not stress rational objectivity as a standard of theological reflection. We do not question that rational objectivity, as a theological standard, has value. But we must recognize that we have been victimized in so many ways by those who claim to be rationally objective, that we must remain highly suspicious of such claims. Who is capable of assuming an "objective point of view"? No one. All points of view are partial and interested. We would rather our bias be explicit and work hard so that our biases fit our intention to be faithful.

Clearly, we must recognize that our passions and commitments can blind us, and contrary to our best intentions, make us turn a deaf ear to the legitimate claims and needs of others. Some level of objectivity is essential if we are to counterbalance our propensity for undue self-regard, and our unwillingness to attend to the needs of those whom we see as other or as our enemies. The best way for us to be vigilant is to work for the empowerment of those whose voice is different from ours. This commitment, and its practical actualization, will help us be attentive to those whom, for one reason or another, we tend to disregard.

However, we believe our bias for the oppressed provides an effective way for all of us to see more clearly some of the exploitative and domineering acts and practices we have become so accustomed to, which we unquestionably take for granted. Our bias enables us to listen to the oppressed, to hear their cry as a first step in denouncing evils and in mobilizing forces to overcome them. This is the way we fulfill two central purposes of theological reflection: (1) denouncing that which violates God's purpose, and (2) calling the community of faith to obedience and commitment to the creation of new possibilities of life. Our theology is partial and passionate, not because we are Hispanic, but because we believe that the God of Scripture is also passionately partial toward the oppressed.

The good and the just are too important to be relegated to a field called ethics or theological ethics. What is good and just is derived from our shared understandings of the nature and purpose of God as these are articulated in the theological themes of the Trinity, creation, theological anthropology, eschatology, and the church. Thus, let us now examine some of the theological views that lie at the heart of the ethics of care and that define the moral vision of Hispanic Americans.

The Vision of God

Hispanic Americans are neither moved nor prone to talk of God in abstract impersonal terms. It is not that descriptions of God as Being itself, omnipotent, omnipresent, immutable, impassible, and the like are alien to us. We use these and related terms in our theological discourse, but these are not the dominant terms with which we normally address the God of Abraham, Isaac, Jacob, and Sarah. Our notions of God express our deepest understanding of ourselves. God created us, redeems us from sin and its consequences, and empowers us, here and now, to pursue new possibilities of life. All that is has its beginning and *dignity* in God. Our *dignity* comes from serving God's purpose of love and justice as this is particularly, but not exclusively, directed to the poor and powerless. Meaning and purpose are found in transforming all that diminishes the dignity of God and God's creation.

Hispanics harbor a strong sense of the transcendent and providential nature of God. That God is transcendent does not mean that God is far away. It means rather that God's freedom is powerful and capable of influencing every sphere within history. Our God is close and personally related to us, and we are personally related to God. When we speak of God, we stress God's care, God's concern with our suffering, and God's desire for our well-being. God is our companion and comfort on our journey of faith as we endure the struggle to create a more inclusive and humane world. Our God is a someone. God is not an impersonal reality, but a personal being whom we experience as related to us not only in the intimacy of prayer, but also at times of fiesta, joyful thanksgiving, and, of course, in our pains and struggles against what makes us suffer.[4]

The importance of the distinction between a philosophical god and a personal God became vividly clear to me during one of my visits to Central America. While in El Salvador I met a human rights activist who vividly narrated to me how he had been subjected to torture by the Intelligence Agency of his nation (which, as we know, was supported by our own CIA). One of the things that he will never forget about this inhumane ordeal was the manner in which the officials who interrogated him warned him about continuing his human rights activism. They assured him that they would hear everything he said and know everything he did. They wanted to impress upon him that they were ever-present, all-knowing, beyond change, and apathetic to his struggle and claims. After a moment of silence he said to me, "I used to believe that only God was all-knowing, impassible, omnipresent, and omnipotent. God cannot be this way if these 'criminals' are this way."

There is something theologically insightful and essentially correct in his story. To describe God as omnipresent, omnipotent, and immutable in abstraction from the life-giving and caring God revealed in the Gospels, is a way of justifying the status quo and the arbitrary and coercive use of power needed to preserve our present unjust state of affairs. This is an idolatrous God at the service of a particular political order which allows some individuals to be sacrificed for the well-being of others. If an oppressive intelligence agency can understand itself as all-knowing, omnipotent, and omnipresent power, then surely God cannot be so described! Politically speaking, immutable, rigid, irre- versibly assigned social roles deny God's free relation to creation; and they diminish human dignity by allowing superiority over others and making some subordinate to the powers of others.

The personal God we Hispanic Americans encounter in Scripture and proclaim as the center of meaning and purpose of our lives, is the God who gave God's Son so we can all be saved; the One who listens to the cry of the people, who recognizes and relates to them, and who is willing to change when we request that God be more patient and forgiving toward us. Our God would rather suffer with us than use power in a coercive or oppressive and domineering manner. What is unchanging in God is God's steadfast love and care for us. Our jealous God never gives in completely to jealousy and frustration with our unfaithfulness. In spite of our shortcomings, God promises us that God will never abandon us. If we are to understand God as all powerful, it can only be in the sense that nothing will stop the ultimate fulfillment of God's just and loving purpose, and that nothing will separate us from the love of God (Rom. 8:35-39).

Our God is loving. When we claim that God is love, we confess our belief in God's power to reunite that which, though created for unity and harmony, has been separated by the coercive use of power. Love is at the foundation of reality and embedded in every effort that strives toward unity. God smiles upon us, then, whenever we move toward the creation of more inclusive and just relationships. Humanly and politically speaking, love entails mutuality of care. The more inclusive and broader our love, the greater the mutuality within the human family. Sacrificial love, the giving of life so others may have life, is ultimately for the sake of recognizing the need of mutual life. Mutuality is what enables us to sustain life for all. Whatever we do or create that fits God's loving purpose will endure; this is the way God manifests God's power.

The unity that results from God's love, as we can witness in all authentic personal relationships, is neither sameness nor is it static. It is a living, dynamic unity which embodies diversity and nourishes differentiation and otherness. If we were to use a paradoxical image or vision, God's love is a kind of *frictionless harmony* where a plurality of parts preserve their differences, but coalesce and work together to give one another life. This vision informs our sense of marriage, family, friendship, and communal loyalty where the purpose is not for all to be the same, but, in and because of differences, to contribute to mutual growth and well-being. Love makes space for and gives a voice to otherness and differences, including them in the shared community in which the equal dignity of all is recognized. Love overcomes sin; that is, it overcomes the fear and hatred of the other, a difference which motivates conquering and subjugation, rather than nourishing and contributing to mutual well-being and growth. Our loving God is powerful enough to be vulnerable, be willing to change, risk being rejected and told no! and suffer. When we posed the question, "How can you believe in God in the midst of all your suffering?" to a group of Central American students, they replied, "Our God shares in our suffering." God's suffering is God's strength and a sign of the ultimate realization of loving solidarity.

Hispanics tend not to use explicit trinitarian language, but we do have a fairly strong trinitarian understanding of God. We also have a preference for what we have defined academically as the *economic trinity* over the *immanent trinity*.[5] For most of us the activities of God have priority over the distinction of persons in God's being. Still, as we will see, both are relevant.

God's love begins with creation itself. Creation itself is an act of the Father's love. It is humanly and politically enacted in the world by Jesus, the Christ, who reveals love as care and service to the poor and marginal, and in his sacrificial giving of himself so that all humanity can have life. And love remains vitally present within and outside the church through the Holy Spirit, who encourages and sustains us in the never-ending struggle to promote love in our personal and collective lives. In creation, God reveals that the purpose of life is found in coming out of self to create and serve the other and that which is different.

God's activities, as revealed in Scripture and experienced by us, define God's inner being as love. God creates "the other," cares for the other in his or her difference and uniqueness, and God seeks community and communion with the other. God refuses to be alone and refuses to use others for merely egocentric or selfish purposes. Rather, God empowers the other so they, too, can be loving and realize their true being in communion and service to others. God's creative power brings forth community even when it seems there are no conditions for community to emerge. God is the new beginner, *the creative agent* who comes out of self so that others can have life, and who wants us to be new beginners or *creative agents* whose freedom is placed at the service of others.[6] Among the deepest longings and hopes of Hispanic Americans is that God will once again, out of nothing, bring about a new beginning so that they, too, can enjoy fullness of life. For us, then, God's inner being reveals itself as diverse Otherness in self-communication and in other-affirming, community-building love.

European Americans, for cultural reasons, have a tendency to describe the trinitarian view of God in psychological language. Hispanic Americans, also for cultural reasons, have a tendency to interpret the Trinity from a sociopolitical perspective. My point is not that one cultural tendency or bias is better than the other, but that they do make a significant difference in our understandings of God. We affirm the essential sociability and communal nature of God and of God's purpose. We lift up communities of care such as friendship, family relationships, small intimate communities, and the creation of an inclusive community of relatively equally empowered social groups as being an imperfect but significant expression of the Kingdom to come. Our God is for the creation of qualitatively new communities, both small and large, in which domination and oppression are significantly reduced, and where the equal dignity of all is recognized and nourished. Such communities are foundations for justice, peace, and freedom to emerge among people of different cultures, races, genders, and class.

As we mentioned, God as revealed in Scripture has a bias for the poor and powerless, who, we are told, have a privileged knowledge of God. (If this is the case, theological discourse ought to be gauged by, among other things, its capacity for communicating with the poor.) God's option for the poor is based neither on their moral nor on their religious merit. In religious and moral matters, the poor are not only not superior, but leave much to be desired. God chooses them because such is God's free, gracious will. It is a choice that speaks more of God's graciousness than of the deserving nature of the elected ones. It is also a way of making clear that God can choose to reveal Godself wherever and to whomever God desires. A consequence of this claim is that, if we truly want to find God, we must find God not where we choose, but where God dwells, among the poor and powerless. God's choice, thus, does not in principle exclude those who are not poor. It is a bias and choice that ultimately leads to inclusion—inclusion not on our terms but on God's terms.

God's choice for the poor is a choice to be in communion and provide community for those who are presently denied communion and community. Negatively speaking, the poor allow us to know, in a concrete way, that which is against God's will. In a positive vein, they let us know those things which must be transformed in order for us to act, personally and collectively, in ways that are more fitting with God's reuniting love. It is the poor, therefore, who most clearly reveal to us the condition of our sinfulness. And their inclusion, as creative agents, in the process of bringing about a more just social order, is a clear indication or announcement of the present and still-to-come Kingdom.

To be privileged in God's sight, however, entails the undertaking of significant historical responsibilities. The chosen ones enjoy no special advantages and securities; rather they are entrusted with the special task of struggling for the creation of a more humane world, that is, to be the good news to all peoples. To be chosen is also to recognize that we have been elected as a people, not as individuals, and that we will be redeemed as a people. So, we are not to separate ourselves from our community, nor are we to separate ourselves as a racial and ethnic group from other groups. We must affirm our particularity and be authentic to the uniqueness of our being as one expression of the creative richness of God. We must also acknowledge that we can only be true to our uniqueness in dialogue and in relation with and in service to others. We are elected to live and contribute to the well-being of our life together.

Even though we are an oppressed and dominated social group, Hispanics recognize that we are not defined by our oppression. Our identity is shaped and our dignity realized through suffering love and loss of innocence, but never a hardening of the soul that would prevent us from struggling for the creation of a better world for all people. In this sense the authentic hopes of the poor have eschatological significance for all people, not just for the poor.

The elected are not only subjected to the same pains and tribulations all historical creatures are subjected to, but also live under God's judgment. If there is something Scripture makes perfectly clear, it is that the elected are not always a happy people. We believe that God creates and cares for us personally and as cultural beings, and affirms our dignity. We are also aware that we must come to terms with the ultimate truth that we are called to exist for God's purpose and not God for ours. Oppressors are not the only ones who try to domesticate God and make God the protector and guarantor of their culture and dominance. We who claim to be oppressed and dominated have similar propensities, although we express them differently. American civil religion and Anglo Saxon cultural supremacy make arrogant claims for God's loyalty, but we make the same claims when talking about the new Raza Cósmica, or mestizo culture. God's judgment allows us to see pettiness and noninclusive tendencies both within our own racial and ethnic group, and in the ways we relate to other social groups. Thus, we confess that we are in need of God's forgiveness because we are not always faithful to God's purpose. We praise God's judgment because it is for the sake of inclusion and election in the community of the saved. If there are people who will not be saved, a matter which only God knows, we believe it will be because of their refusal to listen and respond to God's grace and call for freedom to become community builders.

As we mentioned, Hispanic American theology takes seriously the question of the production and distribution of power. Many biblical stories relate God's calling the powerful to accountability and to stop misusing power, and many stories relate the ways God supports the poor in their quest for empowerment and justice. One of the contributions Hispanics make to the church at large is to keep it aware that its mission goes beyond nourishing our personal faith. Another contribution is to point out that in our present world, being apolitical, as many within the faith community would like us to be, is not a real alternative. Theological reflection and mission work always entail a political option and have political consequences. (We must judge all forms of thinking, theology, and doing, including mission work, in light of their political consequences.)

So-called apolitical theologies spiritualize God and God's purpose to the point of making the quest for justice, if not historically insignificant, religiously insignificant and devoid of redemptive purpose. These theologies attempt to domesticate God and the community of faith and limit our historical responsibilities to narrowly defined spiritual matters. Our theology and mission work become morally passive, insensitive, and irresponsible before the urgent and pressing problems confronted by the exploited and dominated. Apolitical and changeless conceptions of God model for humanity apolitical moral attitudes that cannot but bestow on the present order a sacred quality that blinds us to its injustices. This is the kind of theological vision promoted by those who, on the one hand, advocate prayer in school, while on the other hand they oppose breakfast programs for needy children and bilingual programs for the children of migrants. For them, our children are an economic or tax burden. For us, the children of the poor are a witness to the power of death within our own society and an incentive for us to risk and follow the God of life. They want prayer in school because they believe that prayer is at the heart of character formation and moral action. But their apolitical sense of prayer, and of the God they pray to, allows them to give minimal importance to the fact that our schools continue to be violently segregated on the basis of race and class, and that their policies will make them even more so. These children of piety want us to pray in school but also want us to remain tolerant or silent about the fact that not only are our neighborhoods segregated, but also our churches.

We must continue to raise our voices to proclaim that the God of Scripture is a life-giving God who calls us to promote goodness within all spheres of life, including the political, social, and economic spheres. God's redemptive purpose is not an after-death event, it is very much a historical reality to which we have been invited to contribute. What is truly fitting in God's purpose within history will be there in the ultimate Kingdom in a transfigured and purified way. We must denounce and oppose all spiritualized notions of a god who is distant and does not listen or intervene for the poor. And we must proclaim the true biblical God, the God of love and life who, in liberating the poor, brings life to all of us.

Our sense of a victorious God does not cheapen God's grace, nor is it devoid of judgment. God achieves victory through suffering by our sins, our spiritual sins and the political and economic sins we inflict on one another. All types of sins make God suffer. And because we share in God's suffering, we can share in God's victory. Between creation and redemption there is the cross. God's final victory does not ignore human suffering, but takes it up and vindicates it. Only a politics that frees the weak and powerless of their suffering, that is, a politics that endures in the suffering that such a struggle entails, fits the politics of the biblical God.

In short, the way we understand God has implications for the way we visualize what a just social order is, and how power and wealth ought to be distributed. The communality that exists within the Trinity points to the centrality of mutual recognition and care that is part of God's politics. The normative community of love represented in the Trinity is one of sharing and equality in difference. Life is sustained by love, care, and the sharing of those goods and powers that are needed to replenish and nourish it. A life devoid of care and sharing is a life devoid of the presence of God. Suffering is part of this struggle; it remains a mystery, but it remains real. We are not protected from this suffering, but we are reassured in the final victory of God over the power of death. Our mission as Hispanics is to remind ourselves and our brothers and sisters in the faith of these sociopolitical implications of the Trinity.

Anthropology: What It Means to Be Human

Hispanics confess that our humanity is grounded in our being created in God's image. By the term "God's image," we mean a number of things. First, we mean human rationality or the capacity to think and communicate in universal categories. The conquest and subjugation of persons, races, or nations has been justified by denying their humanity and participation in God's logos.[7] Second, we mean human freedom and the capacity to transform the world through our work. This sense of dominion fits the biblical account presented in Genesis. Creative transformative work is what enables the human not just to satisfy basic needs, but also to create and sustain culture. Third, we mean the human capacity for infinite self-transcendence, which gives us the power to stand back and make ourselves, nature, and all our creations, objects of reflection and transformation. The capacity for self-transcendence makes us aware of our religiosity and our sinfulness. Because we are self-transcendent we are creatures that can find only in God a proper ground for our being. But it is this same capacity that gives us the illusion that we, or one of our creations, can become our own god; fourth, being created in God's image entails that we have the capacity to care, that is, the capacity to come out of ourselves and recognize, listen to, and serve others. Without this capacity we would never be able to understand the providential nature of God's love, or the paradox that life is found when we give it or put it at the service of others. While these interpretations fit what is meant by the term "in God's image," Hispanics understand the notion of being created in God's likeness mostly in terms of the relational nature of human life as a reflection of the relational nature of God's inner being and God's relation to the world.

In our view, humans have value by the mere fact that God created us, wills us to be, makes us partners in the realization of God's purpose, and because, no matter what we do or fail to do, we know God will redeem us and will bestow with eternal life all our creations that fit God's loving purpose. Because we are dependent on and related to God in these three ways, we are bestowed with our unique *dignity*. We have value and dignity through God, but it is our value and dignity.

Theologically speaking, the value and dignity given to us as a gift in the act of creation is ever present and irrevocable. We do not deserve it, and it is not conditional on our doing or becoming a particular someone. We have it just because we have been created by a good God; just by the fact that we are and we are God's. We all share in it equally, the worthy and the unworthy alike, in the same way. And it is ours as the unique individuals we are. In the same way, we cannot ever lose our value and dignity. No one, no matter what they do to us, can take them away from us. Still, this does not entail that it is a matter of indifference how we treat others or how we are treated. There are forms of treatment that do not fit our relations with God's creatures.

Humanly and politically speaking, the value and dignity given to us as God's creatures entitle us to be recognized and treated with respect and care. Recognition, respect, and care demand more than just a change of attitudes and the cultivation of proper dispositions. They entail a concrete transformation of social relationships. As usual, it is easier to point out what recognition, respect, and care prohibit than to specify what they require. Obviously, relations of oppression and domination among social groups do not fit. Individuals, nations, cultures, and social groups are not respected and cared for when some benefit from the contributions of all, and where some are defined in principle as more valuable than others. On the other hand, individuals and social groups are given due recognition, respect, and care when they are assured of what they need to live, can develop their capacities, and become genuine, self-determining beings.

Because we are created by God, each person is entitled to experience the goodness of life itself. We ought not to lack the basic goods of food, shelter, clothing, and health care that sustain us and allow us to experience the joy of our bodily existence. When we confront the plight of the homeless, the poverty among our children, the artificially reduced lifespan of our youth, our school drop-out rate, and our drug-infested neighborhoods, it is unavoidable for us to wonder if we still have the will and capacity to care, or if disdain and disregard have taken over our souls.

But we are not just bodies, we are also complex spiritual and rational creatures. We need goods and services that will enable us to become responsible social and political agents, capable of carrying out what we understand God's call for us to be. Thus, we need a context for meaningful activity, education, and other forms of training that will support our self-development. We need spaces to exercise authority and autonomous self-determination, and the company of others to recognize and evaluate our creations. Participation in the social, political, and cultural spheres that determine the fate of our collective existence is at the heart of being treated with recognition, respect, and care as creatures of God.

132

And finally, given the uniqueness of our being, we need to be recognized and respected for our differences and particularities. Our particular acts, our particular structures of meaning and attachments must also be recognized and cared for. These structures are essential for our identity. Our dignity is tied to our being the particular individuals we are, to the development of our capacities in the company of others, and to expressing our uniqueness in a context of mutual care.

Hispanic Christians tend not to use the language of rights to speak of what is due a creature whose value and dignity are grounded in God's creation. The language is too political and carries with it the connotation of a conflict model of society, in which correct behavior is defined in terms of not interfering in others' lives and making the most of our own independence. We use the language of care because it emphasizes establishing and nurturing new relationships and the importance of our life together. It stresses the obligations we have to attend to the needs of others in a context of mutual and reciprocal concern.

To be human is to be responsive, in an affirmative way, to God's grace and purpose for humanity and the whole of creation. As God's innermost being is communal love and care, so are we to be loving and caring in relating to others. Like the Triune God, to be fully human is to live in harmonious relation with those who are different, to empower them in their difference, and to create community with them. We are most human when the other's need and well-being are taken into account as we go about enhancing our own. The human finds true self in the process of reconciling and reuniting that which has been selfishly and forcibly kept separated. This reunion of the separate, which is what love is, is intrinsically intertwined with justice, or the creation of social structures that enable us to relate to one another in a context of mutual aid, recognition, and respect. To be for the other means more than just not interfering, it means caring for them in positive ways, just as we care for our parents, our children, and our spouses. Being human is to be caring and other-directed within all spheres of life.

We live in the tension of being spiritual and natural creatures. Although we are free and self-transcendent beings, we recognize that we are also finite and subject to nature with all its vicissitudes. Although we are natural beings, we recognize that we are also self-transcendent and free, and as such, creatures who are significantly less subjected to and ruled by Nature. We are endowed with a tremendous capacity to re-create our personal, social, and natural world. We know our creative powers are limited, but we are not able to establish beforehand what the limits of our creativity are. We are called to live within the tension of our natural and self-transcendent being, recognizing that we are created as a unity and for unity.

Many Hispanic Christians still uphold a dualistic notion of humanity and creation. Those who do so tend to argue for a hierarchical ordering of spirit, reason, and body. They also tend to be uncritical of the political implications of their dualistic and hierarchical theological conceptions. They do not seem to understand that hierarchical structures and rigid social roles deny God's free relationship with creation. They are also oblivious to the fact that what is made theologically normative can also become politically normative in the same way that what is made politically normative can become theologically normative.[8]

Dualistic conceptions of the human and apolitical notions of God make us overtolerant of the material or physical suffering of others. As long as its soul is being properly cared for, the needs of the body are devalued. Socially speaking, they do not see any problem with manual labor being poorly compensated and white-collar work overcompensated. Nor are they disturbed by the fact that women and people of color, who are, overall, locked into jobs that are physical or body-related, are paid less than whites who carry the mental, intellectual "burden" of society.

Fortunately, Hispanic Christians are beginning to question and denounce as unbiblical all attempts to speak of the soul as our true being, and our body as being of less value. We no longer see our body and soul as two independent parts of the self, but as two perspectives from which to look at the self. To be human is to live through, not resolve, the tension of our being natural, self-transcendent creatures. We are always both, and without either body or spirit we would not be the particular beings we are.

It is indispensable that we nurture our intellectual capacities as much as our bodies, and that we care for the maintenance and perpetuation of culture as much as we care for the well-being of the natural order. No one ought to be deprived of bodily health or psychological or spiritual well-being. It is *not* that we need a healthy body to develop a healthy mind, or that we need to care for nature for the sake of human well-being and cultural growth! The biblical point is that God called nature good; it is good in itself and not just good for humans. We must care for our bodies and for nature because they are in themselves part of God's good creation. This is why we confess that we believe in the resurrection of the body.

Whether or not one is intellectually bright, whether or not one can think a creative thought, no one and no social group should, because of the pain and suffering inflicted on them, live constantly reminded of their bodily existence. Liberation from the aches and pains of the body is itself enough justification for the creation of a new state of affairs, but we are reminded of the urgency of creating a new state of affairs when we recognize that, in God's eyes, our bodies are an intrinsic part of God's good creation, and an essential part of our being and sense of dignity.[9]

Our native ancestors, who have always been aware of our unique kinship with the earth, know that our relationship with nature affects our relationships with one another and with God. Our technological zeal and its accompanying insatiable desire to consume have affected the way we interpret God's permission to dominate the earth. We assume a carte blanche invitation to exploit and possess all the resources of the earth. Native peoples and religions more respectful of nature, allow us to reread biblical stories and rediscover that dominion is more an act of stewardship than of conquest. Our dominion is to be subservient to God's caring for God's creation. We have to dominate nature in order to become the unique creative agents we can be. But if we must *have* in order to *be*, we are not to *be* in order to *have*, as our consumerist culture encourages us. Whether or not nature has rights, we have the obligation to care for it; whether or not we benefit from nature, we are to care for it just because it is part of God's good creation.

As native people have helped us see the oppression and domination we inflict on nature, Hispanic American women are enabling us to see the gender bias of our present social organizations and personal relationships. Hispanic women are rereading and reinterpreting biblical stories in ways that unveil patriarchal bias and disclose more clearly what ought to be normatively human. God created us in God's image as men and women. As such we are created as social and for social relationships. To be human is to be joined in relations of fidelity and mutual cooperation. It is to live by the medium of dialogue, by listening to one another, by recognizing and respecting one another, and by serving one another's needs. To be human is to have the power that allows each to name their world and their being.

When we name others, depriving them of the power to name themselves, and make them in our likeness, as Adam does to Eve after the Fall, we move from mutuality and creative freedom into domination and oppression. In the act of naming Eve, both Adam and Eve lose their capacity to be for the other, to recognize, respect, and care for each other, and thus their capacity to be truly human. Both Adam and Eve lose their helpmate, that is, a helper fit for ourselves and necessary for our mutual self-realization. To be a helpmate does not entail subjection. We are to be each other's helpmate in the same way God is the fitting help of Israel. Thus, woman is not a subordinate but a counterpart of man's humanity, and man a counterpart of woman's humanity. In our social context the quality of our humanity can be measured by the way we personally and socially treat women and children.

As self-transcendent creatures we are aware that we are incomplete and unfulfilled beings. Consequentialist modes of ethical thinking are grounded in our being forward-looking and forward-oriented creatures. We are through and through culture-creating, meaning-bestowing creatures; we are historical creatures committed to the realization of higher possibilities of life. We have a task to do, assisting God in ordering and nurturing God's good creation. In this task we find not only emotional and material well-being, but mainly meaning and purpose. To be human is to be committed historically to acting in ways that anticipate and give us glimmers of God's Kingdom of love and justice.

In fulfilling our calls, we affirm our differences and particularities. From here emerge a plurality of cultures and systems of value and meaning. In respecting our work as part of God's creation, we must also respect and care for the particular way we express it. Our creations are valuable to us and as such ought to be respected and cared for. No one can be other than who he or she is called to be. To force others into conformity, to establish narrow and rigid boundaries of inclusion, are all ways to oppress, dominate, and violate God's call for inclusivity, care, and recognition of differences. It is a way of placing oneself and one's narrow self-interest and interpretations between God and God's people.

Since creatures produce diversity, we are called to respect diversity out of respect for our being created by God. God is too transcendent and magnificent to be reduced to our limited depictions, much less to only one depiction. Respect is not just adapting to or accommodating the beliefs and practices of others. It is a positive valuing of and contributing to their distinctive ways of being. It is actively relating to others, making them part of our network of relationships. It has less to do with supporting social stability and peace, and more to do with justice and inclusiveness, since only within diversity do we unfold more aspects of the magnitude of God.

Respect for differences forces us to give others the benefit of doubt, to, at least in principle, assume that their views are of equal value to ours until proved otherwise. It is to respect as valuable what other people decide in light of the best of their traditions. We need neither value commonness nor the creation of a greater organic unity between diverse groups to exercise respect. What we need is to recognize the other as other, and rejoice in the diversity of God's creation.

Sin

Sin, for most Hispanics, is not a mere doctrine, it is the way we experience life on a day-to-day basis. Sin manifests itself within social practices, including the accepted laws and moral regulations that allow some to live and prosper at the expense of others. Laws that allow the powerful to accumulate land and to move their centers of production outside communities that depend on them to survive, are means of sin in spite of their legality and accepted morality. Rights that allow people to be indifferent and unconcerned with the suffering of others may constitute acceptable morality, but still embody sin. In fact, what is legal and accepted as moral has the capacity to be more sinful precisely because of the goodness it pretends to have.[10] This is why Scripture makes it clear that we should not be quick in equating the good with order, nor find comfort or security in what is legally and socially accepted moral behavior.

Order, both political and moral, is good, but it is a means of sin when it favors some at the expense of others. Nor can we act on the basis of conscience, since conscience itself is very much shaped by the social world we live in and the social position we occupy within it. From a biblical perspective, conscience is contaminated by our undue self-interest, and thus is more an instrument of sin than a deterrent. It is as much in need of redemption as our passions, feelings, and reason. Whenever laws and standards of morality contribute to the death, physical or spiritual, of others, they are not beyond sin. Christians have a long-standing tradition of civil disobedience precisely because we have always been aware that the legal and the moral are not above sin.

Sin is not to be identified with ignorance, although ignorance helps sin consolidate its power over us. Nor is sin to be identified with the finite and natural dimension of our humanity, although our natural appetites and inclinations can become occasions to sin. Nor is sin ultimately grounded in the unjust way we have structured our collective existence. Rather, immorality and injustice reveal the depth of sin, our personal enslavement to the powers of evil. We are so dominated by sin that ultimately only God's grace and power can free us from this radical misuse of our freedom, and redeem us to be what we were created to be.

We sin because we refuse to depend on and trust in God. Our sin makes us abandon God's vision and will that life be found in service to others. Sin is manifested through our unwillingness to keep God "the radically Other," as the center of our being and acting. As a consequence of this act of undue self-reliance, we use our powers in ways that negate our need for and dependence on "the relatively other," our fellow human beings. We reject the *Other*, and *others*, because we are fearful, selfish, and have an aversion to what is different from us.

Sin manifests itself in various ways. Among those who wield power, sin usually takes the form of human pride. Their privileged positions give them the inclination to claim more power, security, and authority than they are entitled to. They assume forms of perfection that go beyond what is fitting for God's creatures. And given their power, they can exercise and make concrete their arrogant claims that something other than God, for example, their culture, nation, race, and power, is our ultimate center of loyalty and meaning. The powerful give themselves undue self-importance, and come to believe that they have the right to subordinate the claims of others. They assume the freedom to sacrifice those who do not fit or conform to their views and ways. Their economic, political, and cultural power deceive them into making claims of undue autonomy and self-sufficiency, and they come to believe that though others are accountable to them they remain unaccountable to others.[11] Sin is exemplified in the ways they effectively use their freedom and resources to dominate and oppress, that is, in ways that deny recognition and respect for others.

The powerful do not have a monopoly on sin, nor are the poor spared or beyond sin. Within oppressed groups, sin manifests itself through decisions to adapt, justify, and contribute to the perpetuation of those practices and structures that keep them in a state of oppression. If the powerful value themselves more than they are entitled to, the poor tend to engage in self-deprecation or self-hatred. In their sin, the oppressed seek security in the present order, no matter how fragile and unjust, and avoid and refuse to endure the risks and pains that come from being obedient to God's call for justice. They sin when they adapt to the paternalism their oppressors exercise over them, and conform themselves to the few menial activities they are entrusted with, that is, when they make oppression agreeable and part of God's will for humanity.

When the poor surrender their responsibility to denounce the injustices committed against them, they, too, become unaccountable to God and others. Submission to oppression and domination leads to attitudes of self-hatred and rejection of one's group and heritage. It reduces us to being mere victims and feeds our sense that we are incapable of transforming those conditions that make us feel and be less. Theological constructions that proclaim a god alien from, and even opposed to, the legitimate struggles of empowerment of the weak, their struggle for cultural affirmation and social recognition, contribute to the sinfulness of the poor. They depict oppression as natural, inevitable, and fated.

Thus, whenever the church encourages the poor, in the name of the virtue of humility, to accept and adapt to the condition of oppression and domination they are subjected to, it contributes to their sinfulness and betrays its mission of being good news to the people. At times the church forgets that we are called to be humble only before God and to live according to God's will. We are not to humble ourselves before others, much less adapt to their inhumane practices. When we humble ourselves before others we show fear and lack of trust in the trans-forming and creative power of God's gracious love for us. To choose to remain silent when we are abused is a sin; not to struggle to avoid the many pains that are part of it is a sin. It makes us alien to God's will and perpetuates our mutual dehumanization, that is, the dehu-manization of ourselves and of our oppressors. Obviously we cannot always create better possibilities for ourselves and others since the power of evil at times is stronger than we. At such times the most we can do is to resist in the best way we can. What we cannot do is affirm oppression and domination, and deny the freedom and creativity God gives us for the creation of God's kingdom.

Whether from a position of power or of powerlessness, sin consists of our refusal or unwillingness to work creatively for enhancing mutuality and freedom within the conditions of finitude. We are too prone to believe that there is little we can do, and even more prone to believe that whatever good we can actually bring about does not really matter, nor make a significant difference. There are, given the violence and indifference that permeates and dominates all spheres of life today, good reasons to be cynical and pessimistic. Still, it is part of our religious consciousness that we are heirs of a Master who can make the impossible possible. We have been called by our Lord to do that good we are able to do, no matter how insignificant it might appear to us.

This faithful and hopeful attitude, which is quite different from the optimism of our secular culture, is at the core of a life ruled by faith, hope, and love of the God of life. We must recall that for Israel, Canaan was not the kingdom of God; still it was, humanly and politically speaking, preferable to Egypt, and because it was better it was their moral obligation to do what was necessary to get there. For us, too, there is still much to be done once we get to Canaan, but the fact that our Canaan will not be perfect either (that it will not solve all our problems) does not justify our not striving for it. If it is a more caring state of affairs, no matter what shortcomings remain, we have an obligation to bring it about.

We must avoid being both triumphal and pessimistic. The former distorts the goodness we have achieved by making it ultimate and preventing us from continuing our journey toward greater realizations of God's love. The latter also paralyzes us from achieving the relative good we can achieve, by giving up the struggle itself.

I stress the corporate dimension of sin over and against its personal dimension, fully aware that many Hispanics still feel uncomfortable with this emphasis. But we are beginning to question seriously the overemphasis our faith communities give to personal sin and the minimal attention, particularly in our present historical moment, to the corporate dimension of sin. For example, many of us when we think of sinful behaviors, immediately focus on sexual issues. This has merit in that many of our sexual practices are coercive and domineering. Our culture gives an inordinate amount of attention to meaningless sexual gratification, which distorts the purpose and real delight of sexual union as one of the most intense ways we experience the reuniting power of love. Still, the exclusive attention given to sexual sins is being used in ways that veil other public and collective dimensions of sin.

Many who focus on sexual sins while refusing to deal with the political and economic dimension of sin do so because, in their view, economic social and political matters are beyond the competence of the church, or are too mundane and materialistic a concern. Curiously enough, they claim that their views are based on Scripture, but they seem to be blind to the fact that the Bible deals minimally with the regulation of our sexual practices and maximally with the abuse of political and economic power.

Those who advocate these apolitical views, with or without intention, contribute to the privatization of faith. And this is something Hispanics must be concerned with and resist. They must resist because it is a way of giving religious sanction to the dehumanizing poverty and powerlessness in which they live, and because it is a way of delimiting where God is present and where God can be found. If God is sovereign we cannot limit God's jurisdiction and concerns.

One of the contributions Hispanics can make to the community of faith is to keep alive the collective, public dimension of sin, since the personal, private dimension is already overemphasized. Sin has a political, public dimension since at its core sin violates the power of love that calls us to be for and with others. We can also make a contribution by helping members of the community of faith see how the private dimension of life is related to and significantly affected by the public dimension. Even sexual sins have to do with the abuse of power and rendering one of the parties powerless and vulnerable. Spouse (mostly wife) and child abuse, though not exclusively sexual acts of violence, are intrinsically related to the imbalance of power that exists between family members, the lack of self-discipline and limits in the exercise of that power, and the lack of respect and recognition due all members of the family. These seemingly private forms of abuse of power are not unrelated to the public imbalance of power that allows men to concentrate and exercise inordinate amounts of power, and renders women and children virtually powerless. If anything, we need to learn more and be more intentional in our dealings with the public dimension of sin. Ultimately, the political and economic spheres regulate and dominate in the other spheres of life. The possibilities of caring within smaller, intimate communities are dependent on the structures of care that regulate our public life.

Jesus the Christ

Hispanic Christians, like all Christians, identify Christ as the prototype of what it means to be human. But Christ is much more. In Christ we learn both of God's redeeming and gracious love for humanity, and of how humans ought to relate to God. Jesus is single-minded in his devotion to God and God's purpose. He lived the life of devotion to God, "the Other" and of service to "others." His love and care for the different, deviant, and unwelcome affirmed their dignity and sense of worth, and empowered them to live a new life.

At the center of Jesus' message is the proclamation of God's kingdom. He not only proclaims the coming Kingdom as good news but, with his disciples and followers, models the kind of life through which the Kingdom is foreseen in more concrete ways. Life in light of the Kingdom is life ruled by love of God and care for the poor and weak through the creation of a community aiming to live out its compassion. This modeling of a different way gives the world an occasion to change its ways from self-centeredness to regard for others, and from exclusion to inclusion.

The vision of the Kingdom that is at the center of Jesus' message and ministry motivates Hispanics and gives us hope for the possibilities of a better future within history, and perseverance in the struggle for the creation of a more humane world.[12] It frees us to become creative agents because we are assured that God will consummate his purpose of new and abundant life for humanity and that all we create, which fits within God's loving and just design, will endure the perils of time.

When the Kingdom is at the center of our life, we do not need to make one of our lesser creations the center of meaning. Nor do we need to oppress and dominate others to feel secure and in control. On the contrary, we are prone to take the risk of opening ourselves to those who are different, and to include those who are not like us within our sphere of life-giving love. We are also made free to be authentic and affirm the uniqueness of our being, and the uniqueness of those who are different from us.

In Christ we learn what it means to love and serve. To love is to know when to limit our freedom and self-interest, and when to assert it. If at times love calls for self-sacrifice, it never calls for servility and humiliating self-denial. Humiliating ourselves before others is not the purpose of love. Love is a standing by and with others, making God's redeeming and liberating purpose present for all of us. When we love, we do not act out of a cold sense of duty. We perform our obligations toward others joyfully and with a warm sense that what we do is merely a response to the one who includes us in His or Her liberating and loving grace. It is not a sense of duty to a stranger that rules over us, but our being grasped by the loving care of a benevolent parent that fuels our care for others. To love is also to endure the pain and work needed to create, transform, and sustain life-giving communities of

143

mutual help. Love becomes justice when we struggle to reunite the marginal and the poor to the re-created community that allows us to be whole.[13] We can persevere in love because in and through Christ God loves us, and the love we owe others we owe them because God loves them in all their otherness and differences.

For Hispanics, Jesus is our model and teacher; he is our savior and redeemer, the one who surrenders his life for us to have life to the fullest; and he is the triumphant Messiah, the one who conquers the power of death, which discloses his life-giving and life-affirming purpose. While affirming all these visions and understandings of Jesus the Christ, Hispanics are particularly partial to the humanity and suffering of Jesus. As human, Jesus knew the joys of friendship and the agony of losing a friend; he experienced being loved and venerated by friends and strangers, and what it means to be betrayed. He knew how to give the poor hope and be humiliated by the powerful; he knew the emotional and physical dimensions of pain, and the anxiety of dying alone.

Hispanics are attracted to the humanity of Christ because it reveals to us God's steadfast solidarity and care for those who have been made "other" and seen as deviant. Jesus loves the poor in a preferential way, not because they are morally or religiously virtuous, but merely because, given the present religious and political order, they are the ones left out, the ones who have no one to care for them. In a world ruled by sin and inequality, Jesus' love is expressed in a biased way. He exhorts all his followers to give due recognition to and honor the least of these. To make their dignity invisible is to make God's dignity invisible. He reprimands his disciples, his closest friends, when, following the belief of the time that these were people of no consequence, they pushed away the children and women who wanted to come near Jesus. Women and children, the least, the marginal, were the ones to be welcomed, recognized, and cared for (Luke 18:15-17; Matt. 19:13-15 and 18:3; Mark 10:13-16).[14]

But most important, Jesus' suffering and premature death are a vindication of our struggle to overcome suffering. They came about because of a shared perception by the dominant political and religious leaders that he was subverting the prevailing religious and political configuration of power. Religious leaders felt he was undermining the authority of the Temple that provided safe haven for the community against their conquerors. They were offended by the way he publicly shamed them, made them lose face, and undermined their religious authority. Their fear and anxiety was such that they felt compelled to put an end to his life. His Kingdom language was also suspect to holders of political power. It had the ring of subversion at a time when the political mood was conflictual and volatile. Those who helped the seat of political power could not hear, nor could they understand, a politics ruled by a vision of love and care rather than conquest and coercion. Through the same acts by which the powerful rejected and legally killed the one who stands for God's love for the poor, it is revealed that the rejected ones of this world are God's chosen ones.

Jesus is both religiously and morally normative for us. He stands out as the model of the new humanity we long for, that "new person" fully committed to loving God and loving others. He reveals and models for us that life is gained when it is placed at the service of others, and that real power is allowing others to have life. Jesus is so committed to a service of care, that even in his death he assures us that he is merely going ahead of us in order to prepare a place for us (John 14:1-6).

Jesus lives through the tension of his humanity and divinity, neither overpowering nor making relative the other. The essential unity of his humanity and divinity expresses in concrete ways that "frictionless harmony" with which I described God's inner being. If his humanity allows us to identify our innocent suffering with his, his divinity gives his suffering redemptive power. When Hispanics confess that God is in Jesus, they also raise the question, Doing what? God does not merely dwell in Jesus, but through Jesus is emancipating humanity and liberating us to become agents of the Kingdom of peace and justice where we all will have life in abundance. In Jesus God is with us, redeeming us, so that we can become truly human and committed to God's life-giving project.

When we considered the notion of God, we pointed out that there are ways of distorting it that lead us to make the idolatrous claim that God is merely the guardian and protector of *our* nation, culture, or ethnic group. *Our* order and way of life become sacred. No room is left for criticizing the present order, much less changing it. Humanly and politically speaking, we are deprived of engaging in historical processes of change that seek to improve the lot of the less fortunate members of society. Theologically speaking, we deny the freedom and transcendence that is God's. There is a similar danger when our loyalty to Christ leads us into *christological reductionism.*

For many Hispanic Christians, Christ has become the exclusive focus of their faith. They come to believe that the only purpose of religious life is to experience a close and intimate relationship with Jesus the Christ. It is enough to confess that one is born again and to accept Christ as Savior. In so doing, they secure personal redemption. This vision of Christ devoid of God's active historical purpose has the political consequence of making us historically irresponsible.

One of the contributions we can make to the life of faith is to keep the question, What is God doing in Christ? at the forefront of our spirituality. Then we will be able to confess that our Christ is the Christ of and for the eschatological kingdom of God. It is Christ's commitment to God's kingdom that enables us to identify him as the Son of God, and which enables us to identify the gifts of the Spirit as God-given and Christ-given.

The dominant church has a bias for Christ the triumphant Lord. Christ is viewed as the Lord of power and glory. The church of the poor, on the other hand, speaks of the suffering Jesus, the one whose body is pained and flagellated. Christ's suffering is a judgment against the sin of the world. Mostly, the suffering Jesus is the one who accompanies those whose bodies are broken by the power of injustice. We need both the suffering and the triumphant Christ. The suffering Christ keeps us restless and aware of the need to continue to strive for the incarnated love and peace of God. The triumphant Christ motivates us to continue to struggle and to endure in what seems to be an impossible task. Christ triumphant reminds us that our struggles for peace and justice will ultimately be vindicated and that suffering is not ultimate. We are also assured that no matter how short we fall, God will transform and complete what we could and cannot do. The triumphant Christ does not make us comfortable with what is, but frees us to be agents of God's peace and justice which can be. We neither accept the injustices of the world nor carry the burden of change on our lonely shoulders. We strive for the best we can do, but acknowledge that our ways are not God's ways, and that we must depend on and trust in God's transforming and redeeming power.

Thus, the Hispanic vision of God and Jesus lives within the dialectical tension between God's suffering with us and our hope in the ultimate triumph and establishment of God's kingdom of peace and justice. God not only empathizes with us, but empowers us and accompanies us as we move in our journey to create a new world. In God we overcome hate and tribalism effectively and positively through love's power to overcome these, and to bring us into more harmonious communities of care and mutual recognition. This is why Hispanics enjoy life and celebrate and experience community in spite of the oppression and death-giving affronts we confront every day. God is our hope and source of power to overcome injustice in whatever form it manifests itself; in God we are able to endure in our praxis of resistance and positive transformation.[15]

This is at the heart of what Hispanics mean by spirituality. To be spiritual is to live the future that God promises us in the present, even though the life of care and compassion for which we strive seems impossible. A spiritual life is not escapist or irrelevant to the present pains and suffering of the people. It is to live in "burning patience,"[16] confronting the life-denying principalities and powers in the assurance that the God of life will provide and make a difference. It is not so much that we wait for a different reality to emerge, but that we commit ourselves to a different ordering of the reality God has given to us.

In short, Christ our Savior is the one who proclaims God's kingdom of care and justice, and models the kind of life that fits and brings about the Kingdom; he is the one so committed to the realization of the Kingdom that he gives his life so we can see and denounce the violence of the world and find a new beginning toward the creation of the new; and he is the one who assures us that, in the end, no matter how evil and violent the world is, nothing will separate us from God's caring life and the ultimate realization of the Kingdom of peace and justice. In God we find a new historical project: the creation of a new way of being human and of organizing the world so that all may enjoy abundant life.

The Holy Spirit

It would be impossible to conclude this section on theology without making some comments on the Hispanic understanding of the Holy Spirit. First of all, it is necessary to complete our trinitarian conception of God. Second, Hispanics manifest a preference for Pentecostal and charismatic forms of worship in which the doctrine of the Spirit is central. The theological work and insights emerging from base communities, the church of the poor, and all over the world (including the United States), also give much importance to the doctrine of the Holy Spirit.

When we say that we are living under and by the power of the Spirit, we affirm our freedom from those who exercise dominion within the church and within society, and affirm that we, too, have access to the God of life and peace. In the power of the Spirit, people feel the presence of Christ with them here and now. Through the Spirit, we experience within and between us the care and love of God that is denied us within most other spheres of life. The Spirit also sustains our sense of dignity and worth that is stronger and more affirming of our being than anything society can provide and justify. It allows us to be somebody, empowers and gives us the strength to both resist and transform those negative images imposed upon us by society, and continues the struggle for fullness of life.

Hispanics are attracted to the doctrine of the Spirit because, as it is presented in Scripture, the Spirit represents God's presence within us. In the Spirit we celebrate that we are forgiven and, more important, accepted by God in a personal and intimate way. God is no longer a law-giver or goal-giver, but a personal, caring power that is providentially concerned for us as we struggle in our day-to-day lives. The Spirit also vindicates our struggles to resist injustice and forward justice for the poor and weak (Isa. 42:1-4a; 61:1-4). The Spirit that is upon Jesus is now upon us to continue the ministry of care and liberation for the poor (Luke 4:18). In it is the wisdom and power to remain committed to the historical process and the struggle to emancipate the poor.

The Spirit is a source of transformation who allows us to begin anew. Many Hispanic churches that emphasize the power of the Spirit are presently committed to programs of drug rehabilitation. This is a

148

significant contribution Hispanic churches make to their communities that are disproportionately victimized by this dehumanizing addiction. The language of the Spirit enables them to tell their recovering members that they are somebody, that they can defeat the Evil One, and that they have the opportunity for a new and better life. It is a pity that many of these churches do not recognize, or resist recognizing, the political dimension of this manifestation of oppression and domination. The power of the Spirit allows us to experience and build community; particularly, it allows us to build community with those who have been deprived of the experience of community. Communities inspired by the power of the Spirit recognize the imperative of being inclusive, integrated, participatory, and life-affirming in the way they organize themselves.

Some of us overemphasize the exotic manifestations of the Spirit — speaking in tongues, trances, bodily exaltation — but many more, following the apostle Paul, assert that the central gifts of the Spirit are love, hope, and faith, the most important of which is love (1 Corinthians 13). They recognize that life in the Spirit, both within and outside the church, is revealed through the commitment to welcoming, serving, and caring for others. The Spirit is not bound to any denomination, not even to the church itself, but dwells, abounds, and multiplies wherever there are people forming communities of care, particularly communities that care and are hospitable to strangers. Commitment to the creation of political, social, economic, and religious communities of care and recognition are at the heart of the experience of being grasped by the power of the Spirit.

And still the church does have a privileged relationship with the Spirit; the church proclaims the Spirit and cannot avoid being a witness to the power of the Spirit. The church is the community that seeks to embody, practice, and publicly advocate the will of the Spirit within our world. We must therefore look at the church as a unique moral community which nourishes human dignity and models what it means to be a loving and caring community.

CHAPTER 4

THE CHURCH:
A COMMUNITY OF RESISTANCE,
A COMMUNITY FOR
HUMAN DIGNITY

Introductory Comments

In this concluding chapter I argue that the new religious ecumenical movement emerging within the Hispanic community and the social journey and experiences of Hispanics provide an occasion to understand the indispensable necessity of the church[1] for Christian life. They remind us and enable us better to understand why, for so many centuries, confessing Christians proclaim that we "believe in one holy catholic and apostolic Church,"[2] and that what the church needs most of all is to be the church.

In order to be the church, the faith community must go beyond concerns of institutional politics and administration, and reconstitute itself as a community of resistance. The church is called to resist, within every sphere of life, that which violates God's will and purpose for creation. It must resist the powers and principalities that tempt her, in her internal life, to be other than the kind of community she ought to be. And the church must equally resist accommodating itself uncritically to the values and ways of our culture and civil society. Being a community of resistance will allow the church to lift up its commitment to human dignity as an integral part of its response to God's mission to affirm life and to oppose death within all realms of life. Without the resisting church, the affirmation of human dignity will remain abstract, and it will be ineffective without the concrete witness of local communities which seek to make it part of their internal life and a model to society. In the absence of these communities, human dignity remains a lofty ideal removed from the dynamics of everyday life.

Theologically speaking, God created the church with the goal of establishing harmonious communal relationships within all spheres of life. The church is to model within itself and to the world Jesus' redeeming and reconciling ministry through which God's purposes come to fruition. In Christ we are assured that life within all the spheres of existence is being brought into communion with God. The Holy Spirit is presently at work within the church and in its mission to the world, visibly manifesting itself whenever life-sustaining communal bonds are established between formerly conflicting and separated elements of creation.

The church is indispensable and necessary not only to keep alive the memory of Christ, but also to contribute to the historical task of bringing to completion the new and all-inclusive community begun by God (Eph. 2:11-22). The church was founded by Jesus for the purpose of showing the world a different way of living together as a community of mutual support and care for all God's people. This is why it must be internally organized in ways that reveal its commitment to enhancing the life possibilities of all people and visibly honoring their dignity. The church, however, does not exist for itself, but in solidarity with all people of goodwill, and it must contribute to God's purpose by encouraging the creation of structures of solidarity and mutual care that enable us to live a dignified life. In spite of its flaws and shortcomings, and there are many, the church remains the bearer of the historical project initiated by Jesus to give and sustain life to all God's people.

In this vision of the church, a commitment to justice for the poor and oppressed, those seen as lacking in dignity, has priority over mutual beliefs and orthodoxy. The assumption is made that the church's mission for life — inclusiveness, care, and mutuality — is better served if it keeps its distance from centers of power and focuses directly on the imperative of realizing God's kingdom by serving those who are presently deprived of their human dignity. It does not abandon the wealthy and powerful, but creates a space and conditions that bring them into solidarity with the poor; solidarity is not understood as an idyllic personal quest for perfection, but as a dynamic encounter in which the powerful and powerless seek a communal response to injustice. The true church is constituted by religious people of all faiths and by nonbelievers who commit themselves to challenging, on every front, the power of death that deprives us of our dignity. That is, the church is defined more by the historical project that informs its members than by confession and creed. It is that community which lives within itself and aggressively promotes within its membership the values it advocates for and, on the basis of these values, challenges the political state and society at large to become more inclusive and caring.

An Oppressed but Religious People

Religion matters to Hispanics! We are an oppressed social group and we are also deeply committed to religion in general and to the Christian faith in particular. Our discernment of what fits within God's purpose has a privileged position in deciding how to live our life. We call upon our religious beliefs not only in times of personal or social crisis, but in our day-to-day lives. Whether or not people ought to be forced to work during the Sabbath in department stores, movie houses, the race track, and other similar types of "recreational" activities, are matters we think about on the basis of our religious beliefs. Religion provides the ground for our understanding of human dignity. It informs our conceptions of when life begins and how people should be treated. Thus, when we evaluate laws and policies dealing with abortion, welfare assistance, the withdrawal of treatment for terminally ill patients, or the death penalty, we are heavily influenced by our religious convictions. The issue of whether or not it is proper to participate in politics and, if proper, how to express our political options, is itself determined by religious convictions.

Many Hispanics believe in a God who acts in the most unexpected and creative ways, in ways that can even transgress the limits of nature and the patterns of history. Therefore we rely on the power of prayer as a legitimate and effective way of responding to the individual and social challenges we confront in our lives. Our religiosity is also manifested in our commitment to the church as a worshiping community. We gather at church primarily to experience that transcendent source of being we feel dependent on and accountable to. Public worship—through singing, rituals, the reading of Scriptures, and interaction with brothers and sisters in the faith—also provides visions and guidelines that enable us to make sense of our lives. For those Hispanics for whom church life has become their main activity and commitment outside of work, the church is not only their primary experience of community, but the main source of their moral values. It is a communal context that recognizes and affirms our dignity and allows us to perceive ourselves as beings of worth, in spite of what society tells us.[3]

We believe that religion is good in itself, and that it is intrinsically related to moral goodness. That is why even Hispanics who are not religious send their children to church-sponsored schools. These schools provide their children with a safer and more structured learning environment than the neighborhood schools, but what is equally important for them, these schools initiate their children in the basics of moral instruction and behavior. It is fascinating to see how many Hispanic Baptists are being educated in Catholic schools! The fact that we change denominational adherence, visit and worship with diverse church groups, and actively engage in various forms of syncretism, also points to our conviction of the intrinsic goodness of all religions. For example, there are Roman Catholics and Protestants who attend church in the morning, then visit a spiritualist at night; and many members of "mainline" denominations attend regular morning worship at their church and spend the afternoon listening to evangelical and fundamentalist radio programs. This "range of flexibility" is partly due to our conviction that all religions are good.

Resistance Within the Church

Still, Hispanics are quite critical about the church.[4] Our critiques and complaints obviously have their roots in our being an oppressed people. But as a religiously committed people, our critiques signify neither a condemnation nor a rejection of the church. Overall, we have confidence in organized religion, we trust the teachings of our churches, and we bestow our religious leaders with significant authority and influence in our lives. Our critiques, more than anything else, point to the temptations the church must *resist* in order to keep on being the church.

PRIVATIZATION AND INDIVIDUALISM

Hispanics call on the church to resist the drive toward individualism and privatization that dominates our cultural ethos. We do not want a church that is merely another voluntary association that people join or leave on the basis of how it satisfies their personal wants and needs. In too many of our churches, including Hispanic churches, companionship, community, and life together have given way to an individualized and privatized faith. The value of communal life is an intrinsic part of our cultural and religious heritage. God calls and saves God's people as and in community. It is in and as a community that we share the presence and the empowering and comforting spirit of God. And it is in community that we can discern God's will for us today.

Most of us experience social existence as a state of being lost within a mirage of impersonal bureaucracies. For racial and ethnic groups, this doubt regarding one's social and personal significance is compounded by the various ways our being oppressed and dominated makes the world appear loveless and compassionless to us. A deadly sense of anonymity invades all spheres of our lives; it continuously threatens us with the angst of meaninglessness. Most of our tasks, particularly work, are experienced as depersonalizing rather than fulfilling. Under such conditions we doubt that the language of dignity, which is central to our moral sense, points to anything real at all.

Many of us remember that sense of human dignity and honor of the old days, or the world of our grandparents. Dignity was related to honor and honor was interwoven into the performance of the duties and responsibilities of the social office entrusted to us. Dignity was a matter of distinguishing ourselves from others by our competence and merit in carrying the responsibilities of the institutions that ordered and shaped our public life. Dignity was something that only a few enjoyed. Thus, at present, our perception that we are dispensable, one among many replaceable cogs without recognition in an impersonal productive machine, is an affront to our human dignity.

This experience itself makes it relevant for the church to provide a context where people have the experience of being somebody, and where we are recognized and respected in our difference and uniqueness. The church can and ought to give us a renewed sense of dignity as, or rather because, it fosters personal and spiritual growth.[5]

The church can and ought to affirm the radical sense of human dignity that is part of its proclamation of the good news. The church is a privileged community in which to regain our sense of dignity, because within it we must be *recognized* as a valuable somebody, persons created by the Creator of all that is, so loved by God that God gives God's only son, who is steadfast to suffer so that all of us can have a meaningful life. Our dignity is not given by institutions, including the church, nor does it derive its meaning from any of our actions or social status. It is no longer understood as being derived from social function or the development of virtue, skill, and talents needed to perform them. Dignity is now intrinsic to our being created by God. God bestows us all with equal dignity, not because we merit it, but because God loves us.

It is no wonder that many Christians have a romantic attachment to the "small church." The small church counterbalances the anonymity and bureaucratization that we experience in our daily life. It responds to our longing for community, mutual recognition, and belonging. It allows for those intimate relationships that give us a sense that we exist, that we are valued, and that we make a difference in the lives of others. This is also why large and highly institutionalized churches promote the creation of smaller support and interest groups. These smaller units provide a more suitable context for spiritual and interpersonal sharing of faith experiences, and allow people the recognition intrinsic to our sense of worth and dignity.

However, these smaller communities, precisely because of the dominant social trends, can very easily become therapeutic communities concerned with and narrowly focused on private personal piety and individual growth. If they provide for the legitimate needs of some individuals, they do so without questioning, much less challenging, the ecclesiastical and social structures that keep us separate from one another.[6] This is why Hispanics call the church to live within the tension of its commitment to personal piety and spiritual growth, and the task of Kingdom-building within the more conflictual sociopolitical realm.

The church must resist the temptation to try resolving this tension; otherwise it will alienate individuals from their worldly responsibilities, or deprive those committed to bringing down the barriers of class, race, culture, and gender domination from the spiritual foundation they need to continue this historical project. God not only created us with dignity, but the dignity God gives to us is interwoven in God's life-giving purpose within all of creation. Because of our dignity we are centers of moral decision making and creatures who are given the option to abide by or negate God's will. Neither can the mistreatment of others cost us our dignity, nor can our oppressors or enemies take our dignity away from us.

But our dignity is violated whenever we are treated as something other than moral agents and are deprived of the recognition, respect, care, and the opportunities we need to fulfill the vocations and life plans we choose. Part of our dignity is that we have been entrusted, in our different vocations, with the purpose of contributing to God's providential purposes for the whole of creation. Because of our dignity, we must develop the skills and talents necessary to respond as faithful servants to God's purpose for creation. Our dignity includes being God's representatives in and for creation. It is our capacity for creative action, for enhancing the quality of the life of our community, for mutual recognition, respect, and assistance, that makes us different from the rest of creation. The lack of recognition and equal standing Hispanics consistently experience within European American–dominated churches denies this task and promise, as well as our sense of personal worth and dignity. The experience of being "other" within the church, marginal and passive to its life, denies the purpose and reason for the church.[7]

Our marginality and passivity within the dominant church has contributed to the creation of the racial and ethnic church, which, theologically speaking, is problematic. While the racial and ethnic churches provide us a space in which we can, in the presence of our equals, feel God's presence within the community, the cultural homogeneity of the community in the midst of our pluralistic society points to and makes evident the brokenness of social existence as well as the complicity of the church in this state of affairs. If the church itself is not able to model a diverse and inclusive community, it cannot speak

157

with authority and credibility against the class, racial, and gender prejudices that take place within society at large. Its inability to provide an alternative way of living and relating costs it a prophetic voice. Can the church be the church if it follows the oppressive practice of the culture and resists emancipating the oppressed, recognizing them as equals, and including them as full members?[8]

Fortunately, the importance of community is so interwoven with our religious consciousness and is so much a part of our faith, that at times it makes itself present even in spite of us. In the midst of our radically individualized culture, people recognize and cry out for community. People long for membership in communities also because they understand how the freedom to create and sustain communities of meaning and purpose is part of our sense of dignity. The centrality of community for a truly human life is one contribution our faith tradition has, and continues to make, to our culture. The Hispanic commitment to community is also a contribution we can make to our culture, providing all of us with a concrete context of hope so that the Hispanic cry to resist the forces of individualism within the church and our culture can be heard.

Hispanics also want the church to resist the cultural trends toward the privatization of religion. Faith becomes privatized when it is circumscribed in the sphere of family life, personal options, and strictly religious activity, and severs itself from the sphere of work, the sphere of culture, and the social and political spheres where the larger struggles of life take place. A privatized faith deprives the struggles against consumerism, violence, racism, exploitation, powerlessness, and cultural marginality of their religious significance.[9] A "privatized church" substitutes charity for justice. It avoids addressing divisive social and political issues and limits its concerns to socially acceptable and less controversial ones.

This, as we can imagine, cannot but have an adverse impact on the internal life of the church. It can distort worship, preaching, singing, and the celebration of the sacraments that are essential church practices, and part of its reason for being. Worship, preaching, singing, and celebration of the sacraments are central activities by which the church proclaims the good news of God's redeeming purposes for all of creation and shapes the vision of what its members consider valuable in life. This is why it is so dangerous that they contribute to the *privatization* and *depoliticization* of faith, and become distorted by *ecclesiocentrism*. When, in our singing and preaching, the Holy Spirit is domesticated and confined to the inner life of the church, and salvation is confined to participation in the sacraments and other church activities, we distort the meaning and purpose of common worship. The community of faith is bereft of a historical project, and cannot realize its call to be a servant in the process of creating a more inclusive and loving world.

As the church resists the cultural trends of privatization and individuation of the faith and becomes a community of renewal and transformation within all spheres of creation, it lifts up the dignity due all God's creatures. Our dignity is tied to our being free from all the forces that oppress and dominate us, including freedom from those cultural and religious structures that prevent us from serving others as God serves and cares for us. Genuine worship keeps us aware of God's suffering due to our sinful behaviors within the collective and public dimension of life, as much as due to our sinful behavior in our personal and interpersonal relationships. Genuine worship makes us aware of God's presence within the political, economic, and social spheres of life, as much as it makes us aware of God's presence within the sphere of intimacy and interpersonal relationships. Our critique, thus, is a cry to resist any practice that feeds into a vision of reality in which the secular, particularly in its collective and communal dimensions, is placed outside God's sovereignty.

The vices of privatization and individualism affect Hispanic churches as much as or even more than European American churches. There are too many apolitical, ahistorical, and ecclesiocentric practices within the church of oppressed communities for them to remain silent or be merely accusative of others. These practices make the oppressed accomplices of their own oppression by robbing them of the motivation to struggle for the creation of more inclusive communities within and outside the church. If, as we claim, dignity is tied to our freedom from oppressive structures and freedom to responsibly contribute to the life of others, we are accomplices to our indignity. Church life and activity ought to be one of dignifying more and more spheres of life. Where social relations are oppressive, the respect due creatures created in

God's image is violated. We are deprived not only of recognition, but of the positive respect due us. Hispanics may have a vantage point from which to discern what keeps the church from being the church, but it is clear that all our critiques must also be acts of self-criticism.[10]

OVERINSTITUTIONALIZATION

A community of mutuality and service that also attempts to be inclusive and humane, depends on the creation of internal and external institutions and procedures that make its work effective, more efficient, and responsive. Although organizational processes and institutions are necessary, Hispanics call the church to resist the tendency to become narrowly focused on issues of self-survival and institutional maintenance. No matter how legitimate, institutional concerns must not be allowed, given the kind of community we are called to be, to become ends in themselves. This cannot but usurp most of the scarce energies of the community of faith at the expense of its larger mission of service. Hispanics have come to experience how an overinstitutionalized church becomes stale and petrified.

More to the point, an overinstitutionalized church creates hierarchical structures that stand as large obstacles to communal representation and accountability.[11] Power and decision making are highly concentrated and flow from the top down. Its quest to develop good relationships with other socially powerful and prestigious institutions makes it shy away from actions and programs that, while risky, are necessary to forwarding the well-being of the socially oppressed. It becomes socially conservative and minimally accountable to the needs of the weakest members within the community. Its commitment to the poor is limited to providing social goods and services that fit the public sense of charity, but hardly ever does it take steps toward justice which demand not that the poor be given more, but empowered to be more.

Within the hierarchical church, Hispanics experience the same powerlessness and imposition of silence they experience within civil society: We are equally deprived of the dignity and joy that come from exercising responsibility and being publicly recognized as contributing and responsible members of the faith community; we are made into mere followers of the visions and orders of others; we have limited places and activities (be it Bible study or church governance) to express an original thought or word, or engage in creative deeds. And when we do, we are told that our deeds and words, while interesting, are limited in their relevance to our ethnic group, but do not apply to the whole church. The true church provides spaces where the people, particularly the marginal and poor, can develop skills for critical thinking, can engage in decision making, can be recognized and respected, and can influence the decision-making process.

CULTURAL IMPERIALISM

The church must resist any and all attempts made to identify the gospel with a particular cultural matrix, especially a cultural matrix that dismisses the value and contribution of the cultural heritage of others. Our faith tradition distinguishes itself from others in that, for us, acceptance of a particular culture is not a condition for understanding or living out the Good News of the gospel. The gospel, while transcending and transforming all cultures, is equally affirming of all of them. The gospel is global because it is multicultural. Hispanics have a contribution to make within our social context by making it clear that in order to be Christian, one does not have to be European American. This is still an important struggle for us because of our mission history, and because of the continuing influence and dominance of European American pastors and educational institutions within our community. We still need to struggle against forms of proclamation that make our people feel ashamed and culturally and religiously inferior.

The proclamation of the good news assumes a careful hearing of the cries of the people and an understanding of "their ways." Only thus can the Word proclaimed be a response to the people's longing for salvation, truth, and freedom; and only thus can it become an incarnated Word embodied in specific acts of love that model an alternative community which upholds the dignity of all peoples. A global and multicultural church like ours is indeed in a privileged position to create spaces where diverse people can meet with the purpose of promoting greater self-understanding of their differences. It is in a privileged position as a community of faith, trust, and hope to allow people to listen to one another, and to rethink and transform their cultural and political biases, fears, and prejudices. One can think of few institutions that can affirm, rejoice, and celebrate the diversity of cultures and generations that are part of them. It is also in a privileged position to model how unity, harmony, and mutual aid do not require that people be forced into value commonness or surrender what makes them different.

DEHUMANIZING SERVITUDE

In the context of oppression and domination, the church must proclaim a Word of self-love and service to others.[12] The liberating Word of the church must empower the disadvantaged to defend and care for themselves, and encourage them to serve and empower others. The church must avoid, in words and deeds, legitimating types of service that reinforce a conformist attitude and disposition to be servile and mere followers of the projects and visions of others. The notion of the church as a community of service, sometimes called a servant community, is strongly affirmed among Hispanics. For many of us, the church exists in order to serve and to minister to all of God's creatures and to all of God's creation. But we resent and resist paternalism, that is, those types of service that do things *for* people rather than *with* the people. We resist them because they entail submission and turn service into *servitude*. We also resist all calls placed on the oppressed to give up their legitimate interests. These are distorted and abusive ways of manipulating the example of Christ's self-sacrifice. It is a negation of the true Christian sense of service.

True service takes place both through acts of charity and the more demanding struggles for social justice. Its ground, motivation, and spiritual foundation are in Jesus, the servant Lord, who gives his life so that others may live. But we must always recall that Jesus was servile to God, not to men and women. True service is never a bandage approach to our crises and pains; rather it exposes the roots of human bondage. It entails a call to conversion and struggles for the necessary transformation in people and structures. It aims not only at charity, but also at justice and freedom. True service provides support and encouragement in the struggle against the powers that deprive people of a dignified and full life.

The Church and Political Resistance

We have mentioned that Hispanics must resist the split between the spiritual and the political dimensions of the church mission that continues to exist within our churches. Theologically speaking, God is Lord and sovereign over all of creation. Any attempt to bracket one sphere of human existence and claim that it is not part of the Christian agenda is idolatrous; it is tantamount to saying that another, independent power rules within this sphere. The Christian conscience cannot accept this. Creation is ultimately unified and interdependent. The tasks of evangelizing proclamation, spiritual formation, and community building are inexorably intertwined with a mission understood as a ministry of justice and peace.

However, for those of us who push the church to be true to its political vocation, it is important that we resist the ever present temptation to politicize the church. The church cannot compromise its religious character as the nurturer of Christian life. It must resist identifying a particular social movement, cultural expression, or political option or program too closely with the promised Kingdom. God, not human interest, must remain at its center. No matter how just this interest is, if it becomes the center of our endeavors it will still be an idolatrous expression of the human quest for self-control. Only when God's word of grace and judgment remains at its center will the church authentically fulfill the political task of criticizing all structures and powers that are life-denying. The church must view its political mission as intrinsic to its spirituality, but it must resist the temptation to become insensitive and unconcerned with the nonpolitical dimension of oppression. Still, it is important to keep in mind that Hispanic churches are more prone to being apolitical than insensitive to the personal dimension of suffering.

Hispanics in the United States, particularly Protestant religious communities, do not have a tradition of church-based political engagement. Overall, we maintain clear boundaries between the religious and the political spheres. We affirm the protection of religious freedom, and believe that the state has the obligation to provide and preserve an autonomous space where people can worship as they see fit. At the same time, we also believe in limiting the power of the state in religious

163

matters. What is at stake for the church in preserving its autonomy and in limiting the power of the state, is its own integrity and dignity as a community of truth and honesty. What is also at stake in this separation of the political from the religious, is the church's capacity to be an effective community of resistance, that is, a community capable of presenting an alternative way of life to that enforced by the state and civil society. The church needs and must struggle to preserve a space within civil society to live out its moral vision free from government control.

Clearly, Hispanic Christians who have made a choice for the freedom not to participate in politics have done so for reasons other than theological conservatism. Many believe that political activity is ineffective in improving the well-being of the community and is harmful to religious spirituality. They argue that Hispanics are too ethnically diverse, scattered, and disorganized to constitute a political "critical mass." Politics, in their view, is a luxury not available to those caught in the struggle for mere survival against the oppression and domination under which they are forced to live. It is an investment of human capital and resources that would probably result in some other social group's well-being and empowerment, not our well-being and empowerment.

Another reason that has contributed to our forgoing politics is the narrow and negative view our religious communities have of political activity. To be religious and moral is to live according to principles that, if not absolute, are seriously binding. Religion is intertwined with morality, providing it with its substance and motivation. This is why so many Hispanics support prayer in school. Religion and morality have to do with the recognition and respect due human dignity, with honesty, keeping one's word, loyalty, being dependable, and having the inclination to serve others. Politics, on the other hand, is a morally dubious activity. It is intrinsically ruled by egoism and selfishness. Realpolitik is the antinomy of duty and moral commitment; it condones and sees lying as a fitting practice toward the pursuit of its ends. Political friendships are based on convenience and self-interest, and change as self-interests change. In politics, the interest of my group is the main thing that matters, and whatever must be done in order to satisfy it, including hurting others and disavowing moral practices, can and should be done. Morality, thus, is very much an obstacle and handicap to political pursuits and political survival. Given the experience Hispanics and other racial and ethnic groups have of frequently being lied to and betrayed by individuals and groups within and outside our community, one can understand why many among us distrust the political process.

We are highly suspicious of and distrust those who *politicize* religion. One can physically feel the tension at church when an invited political leader uses the pulpit, the context, time, and space of worship, to push his or her political agenda. The discomfort is even greater when the *minister* politicizes the proclamation of the Word. The common wisdom among many of us is that if we cannot avoid engaging in political work, we should strive to be political outside the church. The church itself should never become engaged in politics, since the uncertainties of political goals and agendas, and particularly the lack of moral restraint in politics, threaten the moral authority of the church.[13] Fortunately we are gradually assuming a more deliberate while disciplined commitment to political matters.

A number of recent events have made Hispanic religious communities question their traditional apolitical attitudes. First of all, third- and fourth-generation Hispanic Christians no longer perceive the secular world as a threat to the life of faith. They view the world as a challenge to be solved and are confident that their faith can transform the world for the better, more than the world can corrupt or impoverish their faith. They firmly believe that church political activity, if done with integrity, can help democratize society by supporting alternative voices within civil society and improving the quality of our social life in the direction of mutual compassion and respect.

Second, there has been a growing recognition that many of the problems that burden our community (unemployment, inadequate housing and medical care, substance abuse, inadequate schools, aggressive consumerism, and the lack of basic security) cannot be dealt with effectively outside the political sphere, nor can they be solved by the church alone. The church has neither the resources nor the expertise necessary to address these issues; it has an important contribution to make as a partner, in solidarity with other people of goodwill, rather than as the main actor. When the church insists on confronting these dehumanizing ills by itself, it runs the risk of becoming a divisive force within society, diluting the political power necessary to make the State assume its responsibility for the poor. What is even worse, the church appears to abandon or be morally insensitive to those in need. Thus, more and more Hispanic Christians, on the basis of wanting to be faithful to the God revealed in the Scriptures, are becoming proactive public participants. They find it legitimate to proclaim the sovereignty of God within the body politic as well as within the church. They recognize that calling the state to live up to its responsibility of caring for the poor is a legitimate religious, while political, activity. The community of faith, as an autonomous voice and movement, can provide all citizens with values and ways of life alternative to those promoted by civil society. And, in so doing, it can make significant contributions toward sustaining a healthy, participatory democratic political order.

In the third place, a number of public policy issues such as abortion, assisted suicides, cuts in federal entitlement programs, cuts in bilingual education programs, fetal research, genetic engineering, organ transplants, proposition 187, and the like, raise life-and-death questions that are at the center of our religious beliefs, identity, and convictions. These issues have motivated many Hispanics to engage the political process, to strive to shape social policy as a witness to our accountability to God.

Another important variable has been the influx of refugees from Central America. Many have brought with them theological and political praxis models of reflection in which theory is at the service of social transformation. They have also brought the experience of Christian base communities, which combine the religious commitments of care and compassion to the poor with the political advocacy to empower the poor. They have experienced, directly or indirectly, how faith communities are capable of organizing morally conscious communities for effective social and political action. While many Hispanics remain suspicious of the political nature of these modes of theological reflection and action, we highly respect their commitment to the study of the Scripture, their advocacy for the dignity of the poor, and their commitment to religious spirituality. Hispanic Americans have not embraced fully the tenets of Liberation Theology, yet we cannot but reveal our hidden and not-so-hidden pride that this theology is a creative and legitimate expression of a faith journey that must be seriously considered by all members of the church. We recognize how appropriate it is for us to incorporate the language of liberation into our pastoral and theological work, since the language and motifs of liberation fit our religious heritage and describe the basic longings of Hispanic oppressed communities in the United States.[14]

Finally, Hispanics have come to the awareness that the refusal to act politically for the sake of orthodoxy or religious purity can be detrimental to both the religious sphere and the political sphere. Religion and morality have an inescapable political dimension. Without some form of political involvement, the moral values that are intrinsic to our faith commitments are reduced, at best, to ineffective preaching or to mere pronouncements that cannot mobilize people or bring about desired changes. Apolitical morals are condemned to invisibility. Moral claims, in order to become an effective presence in our world, must be accompanied by that political commitment that will make them part of the institutional structure that gives order to and regulates our mutual dealings. Institutions have a greater influence over the formation and transformation of our habits and practices than disembodied words. Thus, we have come to the conviction that good ethics is always political ethics.

However, it is precisely at this moment, when Hispanics are beginning the journey to express our political voice as Christians, that we encounter a distressing and confusing reception. The dominant political mood is that people who act politically out of religious conviction are suspect. We are viewed as ignorant and fanatical people who are merely trying to impose a conservative moral agenda by using the coercive power of the State. Religious convictions are identified with the promotion of conservative policies. The dominant liberal establishment does not welcome, listen to, or take seriously (and even submits to ridicule) anyone or any group that acts politically out of religious beliefs and convictions.[15]

Clearly, the liberal tendency to ridicule, dismiss, and even discriminate against those who act politically out of religious convictions is not aimed at Hispanics qua Hispanics. However, insofar as religion is an integral part of our culture and collective personality, and insofar as our religious political voice is mostly conservative or to the right of center on most social issues, we cannot but experience the liberal political establishment as inhospitable and oppressive. Political liberalism repeats to us what our oppressors have always told us: that we are not capable of rational thinking or of responsible public participation, and that we ought to remain within the private sphere since religion is a private and subjective matter, a belief or preference, not a suitable basis on which to determine the destiny of the nation.

But religion matters to Hispanics! It is foundational to our sense of dignity and provides us with direction and purpose in our lives. It is *nonsense* to expect us to respond to issues that matter to us, whether political or not, without the guidance and insights of that which nourishes our spirituality, gives us a vision of reality and how the world works, and informs our sense of how it ought to be organized. Our political voice will inevitably have a religious foundation.

Hispanics are resisting, by political means, the idea that they have to abandon their religious convictions when they enter the gates of politics. This makes no sense to us given that, in our social setting, religious language, images, and visions are not alien or strange. Those who speak with religious conviction and with religious images are clearly understood. However, it is our conviction that we have a right to be heard and to participate politically just because we are members of society. This right to participate in forming and in shaping the community we belong to is, as we mentioned, part of what is entailed in being treated with dignity.

We remember how we have benefited from and contributed to the civil rights and peace movements. Within both we experienced how religious convictions can lead to prophetic denunciation and progressive political options. The liberal establishment must retrieve the memory of these religiously inspired movements, which gave it the power it presently enjoys. More important, given the present political mood, liberals must be careful not to continue pushing religiously committed people into the hands of the politically conservative. As liberals abandon the symbols, longings, and visions of the religious community, they deliver Hispanics into the hands of the conservative political forces that are illegitimately monopolizing religious language. When liberals criticize the conservative political options of Hispanics, and there is much to criticize, they ought to do so on the basis of how the policies proposed will actually hurt the Hispanic community, not on the basis of the policies' having a religious foundation.

Liberals must learn, as liberation theologians have learned, to honor the religiosity of the people. They must recognize how religion is not only an intrinsic part of our dense cultural heritage, but also how it potentially can be a source for liberating political action. There is some truth to the claim that the more religiously serious a Hispanic person is, the more conservative she or he tends to be in social and political matters. Still, it is important to be mindful that this has not always been the case, nor does it need to be the case. That change, while difficult, is possible. As people confront their oppression they can change their political views. The possibility of such conversion or change of heart ought not to be taken lightly. The liberal establishment must recognize that while the religious and the political are interrelated, they are also independent, and religiously conservative groups can be politically liberal and vice versa.

Hispanics, on their part, must continue to resist the cultural tendency of keeping people who work out of a religious frame of mind politically marginal and silent. They must continue to affirm the positive contributions their faith can make to the body politic. There are built-in liberating elements within their religious traditions that, no matter how obscure and distorted they have been made, have a way of resurfacing and calling us all to accountability. The call to do justice to the poor, to honor human dignity, to enhance freedom and equality, and to be loving and caring toward one another, springs to our consciousness in spite of ourselves.

Hispanics, as members of faith communities, can make a significant contribution in creating an atmosphere within the public sphere in which all are welcomed and empowered to speak their minds on public issues, disregarding the basis on which they ground them. They can contribute to the body politic those essential political virtues of listening to, recognizing, respecting, and persuading others. They might be the ones to contribute to these virtues precisely because they have been denied them for so long.

As the church stands for dignity, within the political arena it struggles for the recognition and the concrete realization of human rights.

It resists anything that unduly restricts or violates those human rights intrinsically related to what it means to be treated with dignity. The rights in question are the following: (1) the right to exist and have a decent level of well-being (this entails the traditional rights to food, clothing, shelter, health care, work, decent wages, and the goods and services that allow us to obtain basic well-being. This right is grounded in the fact that we are God's creatures who manifest God's image); (2) the right to self-development of one's capacities (this entails rights to the education and training needed to build one's potentials as one sees fit, and it is grounded in the freedom we receive as a gift of God); (3) the rights of political and social participation (these enable people to have a voice in all matters that affect their lives as workers, members of society, and citizens, in significant ways, and to be recognized and given authority; it allows us to create community and give of ourselves so that others can be free. This is theologically grounded on the promise of the coming Kingdom).

While these rights fit within traditional liberal society, Hispanics emphasize the centrality of community-building, shared life, and service to others which gives these rights their reason for being. Rights emerge from our concrete communal relationships and the new encounters we experience that enable us to get to know strangers and make them part of our sphere of moral concern. They are not so much for the sake of not being interfered with, but for the sake of making us aware of our obligations to others. Rights are for the sake of autonomous action and creative activity, but within a context of mutual aid and support. And they are for the sake of creating an egalitarian society in which competition is for the sake of mutual improvement, rather than the Darwinian conception we presently have, which justifies the oppression of the weak in the name of the progress of humanity.

Rethinking the Marks of the Church

It is ironic that Hispanics encounter discrimination precisely within the two spheres where they expected to find greater freedom and protection for self-expression: the sphere of culture and the sphere of religion. The United States, particularly for the new settlers, was a haven from persecution, a land of opportunity to overcome poverty, a place of freedom to express the uniqueness of their identity, and a nation rooted in a deep sense of religiosity. What Hispanics experience, however, is discrimination because they are poor, culturally different, racially mixed, and, more recently, because their religious convictions inform their political views. These and other forms of exclusion and discrimination create the necessary conditions for Hispanic Christians to rediscover the church as a community of religious cultural and political resistance, and for the promotion of human dignity.

The resistant church, however, as an expression of the true church, must remain one, holy, catholic, and apostolic. For Protestants, these marks of the church center on the Word preached and sacraments shared. That is, they center on the incarnated Word, the ground of all that is true, which promises good news and life to all, and the table to which all are invited just because God loves them. These two elements inform, among Protestants, the classical conception of the marks of the church.

The church is one, but its unity does not entail sameness or uniformity. It is a unity of diversity, diversity of gifts, of race, gender, class, ethnic origin, or even of beliefs and polity. It is a unity of fellowship that affirms and rejoices in the wondrous diversity that God created, and the unique dignity which is intrinsic to all created beings. It is unity as the reunion and communion among those who are different. More than anything else, it is reunion with and commitment to the poor and oppressed. These are the radically other, the ones who have forcibly been kept separate. Reunion with these, the preferred ones of God, signifies and announces the coming of God's ultimate act of reconciliation. The reconciliation, which was given to the church as a historical project, will be completed and given to us as a loving gift from God. All the faith community does to promote structures of care and love, which include the strangers and transform them into members, will endure and be transfigured by the loving power of the community's creator, redeemer, and sanctifier God, and will become part of the promised Kingdom.

The church as the community of sinners that has been forgiven by Christ is holy not in the sense of being morally perfect or superior. The church is holy because it lives by standards other than those of our individualistic and privatized society, by the standards and commitment to communal solidarity, particularly with the ones identified as less and unworthy. It is holy in that it recognizes and uplifts the human dignity of those socially defined as "other." The holiness of the community is found in its willingness to humbly but firmly embrace those who are despised, put down, and abandoned by the dominant culture. True holiness takes place as the church includes the marginal, itself becomes poor, and struggles from its powerlessness to empowerment of those kept silent and made passive.

The church is catholic in the sense of being capable of incarnating itself within the plurality of cultures that provide the various peoples of the world a sense of meaning and purpose. It is catholic in its capacity to be good news to all peoples within their unique cultures. The universal or catholic church is neither culturally neutral nor uncommitted. Its universality is signaled precisely when it is genuinely incarnated within the diversity of particular cultural matrices, without making any of them a requirement for or condition of the way of faith. The church is truly catholic precisely when it is partisan and advocates the inclusion of those cultures and peoples left out.[16]

The church is apostolic when it conforms itself to the witness provided by Christ. This conformity is not the sole responsibility of the clergy or the ordained, it is the call of all believers. It is apostolic when its proclamation of the gospel is also a struggle to live according to the gospel. It is clearly made manifest in the ways it goes about doing its mission and proclamation, not by the means of the powerful, but by the means provided by God; weakness and poverty are used for God's glory and the salvation of humanity. The apostolicity of the church takes place where Christ is among the poor, the imprisoned, the naked, and the hungry (Matt. 25:33ff.). All people as images of God, reflections of Christ, have dignity that has to be recognized and honored.

NOTES

INTRODUCTION

1. Among the best introductory texts to ethics, please see William K. Frankena, *Ethics*, 2nd ed. (Englewood Cliffs, N.J.: Prentice-Hall, 1963); T. Beauchamp and J. F. Childress, *Principles of Biomedical Ethics*, 4th ed. (New York: Oxford University Press, 1994); B. Birch and L. Rasmussen, *Bible and Ethics in the Christian Life*, rev. and expanded ed. (Minneapolis: Augsburg, 1989); and Adolfo Sánchez Vázquez, *Ética* (Mexico: Editorial Grijalbo, 1969).
2. Iris Marion Young, *Justice and the Politics of Difference* (Princeton: Princeton University Press, 1990), pp. 42-48.
3. The ethical work of Anthony Cortese, particularly its ethnic emphasis, is a significant contribution to Hispanic moral thinking. Also see his "Moral Development in Chicano and Anglo Students," *Hispanic Journal of the Behavioral Sciences* 4 (1982): 353-66; "A Comparative Analysis of Ethnicity and Moral Judgment," *Colorado Association for Chicano Research Review* 1 (1982): 72-101; and "Moral Judgment in Chicano, Black and White Young Adults," *Sociological Focus* 7 (1984): 189-99.

CHAPTER 1: HISPANIC STYLES OF MORAL REASONING

1. The categories "oppression" and "domination" as used in this chapter are developed by Iris Marion Young in her work *Justice and the Politics of Difference* (Princeton: Princeton University Press, 1990), pp. 39-65. David T. Abalos also uses these categories in *The Latino Family and the Politics of Transformation* (Westport, Conn.: Praeger, 1993).
2. For specific statistics on this issue, see Leobardo F. Estrada, "Comunidades latinas en los Estados Unidos: Su presente y futuro," *Apuntes* 2 (1995): 35-44. Also see Justo L. González, *Mañana*, pp. 34-35; Ada María Isasi-Díaz, *In the Struggle: A Hispanic Women's Liberation Theology* (Minneapolis: Fortress Press, 1993), pp. 22-28; and Allan F. Deck, *The*

Second Wave: Hispanic Ministry and the Evangelization of Cultures (Mahwah, N.J.: Paulist Press, 1989), pp. 10-12. These authors examine the economic and social conditions of the Hispanic American population and find, with few exceptions, an overall state of poverty, economic stagnation and marginality.

3. The Hispanic American population has traditionally been identified with three main groups: Mexican, Puerto Rican, and Cuban. The census of 1990 reveals, however, that the fastest-growing group of Hispanics coming to the U.S. are those "ingloriously called 'other Hispanics!'" People from the various Central American nations, from the Dominican Republic, and Latin American nations constitute one quarter of the nation's Hispanics. See Blanca Nieves, "The New Hispanic Immigrants," *The Hispanic Outlook in Higher Education* 4 (1994): 1-5.

4. The media has a propensity to describe Hispanics as dishonest, inclined to criminal activity, and as being handy or skillful with knives! We are also depicted as being "hot," crazed with sex; careless and carefree when it comes to family values, discipline, and birth control; and driven by pleasure, dance, drink, and games. Hardly ever are we described as a people that hold two or three jobs to sustain our family, who want and work hard for our children to have a better life than ours, and who suffer the anxiety that comes from the uncertainty of not knowing what the future will bring to them, but who meet our future in struggle and joy and hope.

5. That we have become quite loose and careless with our language becomes evident when we find it possible to describe the ghettos we are forced to live in as a community. To so describe them we must conceal the day-to-day violence experienced by our elderly, the drug culture which kills the life prospects of our children, and the genocide of gang life. The kind of poverty and powerlessness our ghettos represent show that there is, in fact, little possibility of community within them.

6. "As a child Luis grew up surrounded by violence both psychological and physical. To be hit with a belt, a board, a fist, or to have his hair pulled was part of his everyday existence inside the home and in the neighborhood. Racial and ethnic taunts were commonplace. . . . As an aspiring member of a gang, he had to beat the boys from rival gangs to prove himself to his peers. . . . Luis was experiencing the drama of tribalism, the story that tells people who come from communities of color that they are not valuable. As a result he was often physically challenged as a 'Spic'" (Abalos, *The Latino Family*, pp. 67-73).

7. Anthony Cortese, *Ethnic Ethics: The Restructuring of Moral Theory* (Albany: State University of New York Press, 1990), p. 91.

8. The classical expression of Utilitarian Ethics is presented by John Stuart Mill and Jeremy Bentham. A Christian advocate of utilitarian ethics is Joseph Fletcher, *Situation Ethics: A New Morality* (Philadelphia: Westminster Press, 1966).

9. This mode of ethical thinking is known by the technical name deontological ethics or the ethics of duty. The classical formulation of this ethics was given by Immanuel Kant. An influential Protestant formulation of this ethical point of view is developed by Paul Ramsey.

10. At present our political debates center on the issue of whether or not we are to keep or to eliminate guaranteed federal entitlements for the poor. The present political mood is to reduce or eliminate many entitlement programs and to allow the states to determine how to provide for the poor. We are reconsidering going back to a time when only negative rights were recognized. In spite of the institutionalization of the welfare state, many still identify welfare grants not as justice claims, but as charity.

11. Aristotle and Plato provide the classical expression of the ethics of character. Thomas Aquinas and Augustine deal with character formation from a theological point of view. Alasdair MacIntyre is one of its strongest philosophical advocates. See his *After Virtue* (Notre Dame, Ind.: Notre Dame University Press, 1980) and *Three Rival Versions of Moral Inquiry: Encyclopedia, Genealogy, and Tradition* (Notre Dame, Ind.: Notre Dame University Press, 1990). Stanley Hauerwas is among the Protestants who represent this kind of ethical reflection. See his *Vision and Virtue* (Notre Dame, Ind.: Notre Dame University Press, 1974). And William Bennett, former Secretary of Education and Drug Czar, has made character formation central to our present political debate.

12. In a conversation I had with Justo González, he confessed that he never understood Kant. What he meant, of course, was not that Kant's ethics was beyond his comprehension, but, as most Hispanics believe, that morality is more than rational, that it must also have emotional content.

13. Given the individualism that is dominant in the U.S., one can understand the suspicion and fear that exists regarding the tyrannical potential of communal life. The prominent and influential theologian Reinhold Niebuhr notes how groups and communities have a greater propensity for evil. Hispanics are not naive about the dangers of community. But we also know that in the absence of community we are bereft of security, protection, and the possibility of emancipation. Community, for us, is the source of our moral formation, and we need it to keep us within the moral path.

14. Many Pentecostal Hispanics, who were formerly apolitical, have recently come to emphasize the reality of structural oppression through the use of the biblical language of power and principalities. See the work of Eldin Villafañe, *The Liberating Spirit: Towards an Hispanic American Pentecostal Social Ethics* (New York: University Press of America, 1992).

15. Arthur Schlesinger, Jr., as a strong advocate of political homogeneity as a way to preserve the unity, stability, and strength of the nation, is acutely aware of this grave problem. But he provides no solution to the dilemma except to exhort the dominant groups to be more hospitable and excluded groups to accept the status quo. See his *Disuniting of America* (New York: W. W. Norton & Co., 1992).

16. Nothing reveals our social lovelessness more, than our incapacity to care for the young. One out of every five children in our country lives in poverty. The question must continue to be raised: What makes us believe or makes us expect that children who know that no one cares for them will, when and if they grow up, care for us?

17. It is interesting to notice how this movie, which is by far affirming of Hispanic culture and identity, cannot escape typical Hollywood stereotypes. It is common in our media to have a criminally inclined Hispanic bear the name Jesús. Many are the shows that have a Hispanic delinquent with a golden heart called Jesús, and who sooner or later reveals himself as a skillful knife fighter! The popular TV series "Hill Street Blues" also had its stereotypical gang leader Jesús.

CHAPTER 2: STRUGGLES FOR SOCIAL JUSTICE AND THE PLURALITY OF MORAL VALUES WITHIN THE HISPANIC COMMUNITY

1. For too long Hispanics have been engaged in the wrong kind of discussion. We have spent too much energy trying to convince one another whether the Christian thing to do is to witness what Christian social action entails, or to engage in transformative social change. More and more we are coming to realize that we must do both. We have to witness within our churches what a caring, compassionate, and just community looks like, and we have to free the poor and powerless of the forces and necessities that keep them under conditions of domination and exploitation.

2. The term "solidarity" is used too frequently and as a platitude, both of which make us forget the deep-rooted religious heritage behind it. To be in solidarity is to be open to responding in faithfulness to God's good news of revelation to the poor. It points to those concrete political, socioeconomic, and religious commitments to defending the poor. It entails a

dynamic or covenantal relationship which changes and grows as our relationships change and grow, in which oppressor and oppressed recognize each other, honor each other's dignity, and attempt to fashion a response to the injustice we live under for the sake of promoting life among all members of society.

3. I am not pleased with the term "emancipation" but I am not sure if any other term is better. I could use "liberation," but would encounter similar problems. What I want to express is this: that social process through which a people assumes greater control over their collective destiny. It has a never-ending quality to it making us aware of the importance of communal vigilance and self-criticism as a permanent task within the just community.

4. I am creating a typology to help us differentiate between competing notions of justice within the Hispanic community. Typologies are ideal constructions that overemphasize the main traits of a given position. Thus, they always distort the uniqueness and integrity of every particular movement and author. Typologies work best when we use them to determine how a movement or an author both fits and does not fit within one of the types. Most social movements and authors fit somewhere between two of the types, or they will have elements of all the types. Liberation movements, socially radical groups, and progressive community organizing groups would be representative of this ideal type. Also see the distinction between the functionalist social perspective and the radical social perspective made by Allan Figueroa Deck in his *Second Wave: Hispanic Ministry and the Evangelization of Cultures* (New York: Paulist Press, 1989), pp. 21-25. The author correctly states the importance of our taking from what is valuable of every perspective, in spite of the fact that one will be preferable to us.

5. The politics of recognition and resistance among Mexican Americans began after the Treaty of Guadalupe Hidalgo (1850–1915), which guaranteed Mexican Americans their religion, property, and political liberty. But like many other treaties of the U.S. government, it was never enforced. This led Mexican Americans to create *mutualistas* societies. These organizations for mutual aid in some cases led to resistance and even to open revolts. The other significant period, 1960–1974, was one in which Mexican Americans established the La Raza Unida Party. See Roberto E. Villarreal, "The Politics of Mexican American Empowerment" in Roberto E. Villarreal, Norma Hernandez, and Howard Neighbor, eds., *Latino Empowerment: Progress, Problems, and Prospects* (New York: Greenwood Press, 1988), pp. 1-10.

6. It has never been the habit of Hispanics to vote in block. Although they have tended to support candidates of the Democratic Party, there are cases in which they have favored Republican candidates. Today the voting habits of the community are mixed. Hispanic candidates, particularly in the Southwest, who have had successful political careers, have done so on the basis of coalition politics. Coalition politics does not entail that all those who work in concert agree on all matters of principle, belief, and ultimate conviction. Each can have and keep his or her own particular identity and main concern. But if different groups share deeply felt convictions about some issues, they can and ought to be open to working together in those matters that are of common concern. In this vision of political life some degree of organization is essential, but there is no need to have centralized control and management. There is no need to establish a single authoritative perspective or strategy for all members to follow. It is based on mass mobilization, local participation, and grass roots initiatives. It is democratic and participatory rather than hierarchical and authoritarian. Suggestions have been made to build a "Latino Reapportionment Coalition" whose task would be to monitor reapportionments in state and local jurisdictions, to testify at public hearings when there are violations of voting act laws, gerrymandering and the like, to contest discriminatory redistricting, and to conduct educational conferences to offer information and support to representative districting activists (James A. Regalos, "Latino Representation in Los Angeles," in Villarreal, Hernandez, and Neighbor, eds., *Latino Empowerment*, pp. 91-104).

7. Mexican American organizations such as the League of United Latin American Citizens (LULAC), the GI Forum, and the Mexican-American Political Association (MAPA), which dominated Mexican American politics from 1920–1960, are representatives of this type. These are status quo organizations representing mostly the economically mobile and assimilation-oriented Hispanic middle class. This type was mostly conservative until quite recently, when it became more middle-of-the-road. It does represent the "bastion of Mexican-American representation and Chicano empowerment." See Villarreal, Hernandez, and Neighbor, eds., *Latino Empowerment*, p. xxii. In this same anthology, also see Benjamin Marquez, "The League of United Latin American Citizens and the Politics of Ethnicity," pp. 11-24. Most churches and church organizations, mainline or free, conservative or liberal, are also representative of this ideal type. Churches that belong to the Anabaptist tradition or who understand themselves as intentional countercultural communities defined by one stringent moral principle or point of view do not fit this model.

178

8. In this perspective it is important that we nourish and protect civil society from the presence of the state. When it comes to values, it is important that a space exist for voluntary associations to embody, practice, and advocate values. Otherwise values will give way to coerced and programmed behavior and demands of the state.

9. Many political analysts have argued that one reason the Democratic Party appointed Cisneros as Secretary of Housing was to regain the loyalty of its Hispanic constituency and to motivate Hispanics to be more active in national issues as opposed to their traditional concerns for local issues. Other appointments, such as the former Surgeon General Antonia C. Novello, had the same purpose.

10. When I lived in Chicago, whenever community organizers wanted to inform a large sector of the community of an event or action that would affect or take place within the community, they called up a number of Pentecostal pastors sympathetic to their cause to get the word out as soon as possible and to the largest possible number of people. Even though most of the organizers were not themselves religious individuals, they still recognized the church, in spite of all its faults and shortcomings, as a community morally grounded and with moral credibility.

11. In the United States, churches dwell in protected spaces and enjoy a number of privileges that provide them the opportunity to be advocates of a number of morally and religiously based causes, within both civil society and the political realm. It is a pity that Hispanic churches do not use their influence or take advantage of their freedom more frequently to advocate for the pressing needs of their community. Hispanic churches are making impressive contributions in the area of drug addiction rehabilitation. They still view these programs as humanitarian social programs and resist dealing with the political causes that make our community a target of this death-bestowing enterprise.

12. More and more Hispanics are coming to terms with the fact that the option either to change the behavior of individuals or to transform the social structure is a nonsensical one. We need to change both and recognize that individuals change as they change their social world, and that the motivation to persevere in changing the social world needs individuals inspired by vision and courage. We are more and more aware that good individuals within an unjust social setting will act in ways contrary to their beliefs and convictions, and that just institutions will not free us from malevolent individuals who resist caring for and serving others.

13. La Raza movement, the various Chicano community organizing groups that emerged from it during the mid-1960s, and similar groups within the Puerto Rican community, are representative of this type. These movements broadened the political participation of Hispanics by integrating them into the struggle for civil rights. Political participation moved beyond the Hispanic middle class and now includes all sectors of the community. This was also the beginning of a higher level of cultural awareness and cultural pride for all Hispanics. It must also be noted that the Hispanic community was not of one mind. As it became more politicized, the community also became more polarized. La Raza Unida Party in Texas represented the height of politicization among Mexican Americans. For many recent Latin American and Central American groups, Paulo Freire provides an ideological basis for some of the goals of the movement.

14. In my experience with university and seminary racial and ethnic students in the United States, I frequently listen to their complaint that they are treated by other students and some faculty members in ways that communicate to them that they do not belong, that they are there for reasons other than merit, and that they must adapt to the present order of things, since ultimately the institution does not need them as much as they need the institution.

15. See Arthur Schlesinger, Jr., *The Disuniting of America* (New York: W. W. Norton & Co., 1992).

16. Stephen Carter's distinction between toleration and respect is insightful and informative. "Toleration . . . means only allowing someone to exist — but one may exist and still be oppressed. . . . Tolerance without respect means little; if I tolerate you but do not respect you, the message of my tolerance, . . . is that it is my forbearance, not your right, and certainly not the nation's commitment to equality that frees you to practice your religion. . . . And since I merely tolerate, but neither respect nor approve, I might at any time kick away the props and bring the puny structure of your freedom down around your ears" (*The Culture of Disbelief: How American Law and Politics Trivialize Religious Devotion* [New York: Basic Books, 1993], p. 93).

17. For the concept "double consciousness," see W. E. B. DuBois, *The Soul of Black Folk* (Greenwich, Conn.: Fawcett Publications, 1961). DuBois' classical statement of how oppression makes members of minority groups social insiders-outsiders remains relevant for our discussion. Members of underrepresented groups, by incorporating part of the dominant culture, become both "insiders and outsiders" of U.S. society. Their sense

of being citizens cannot disregard the reality of poverty, racism, and cultural distinction that is an integral part of being a U.S. Hispanic. Therefore, they keep the traditional cultural images that enable us to struggle against these forms of oppression. As insiders-outsiders they have a clearer understanding of oppression and injustice found in this society. Also see Cornel West's examination of Malcolm X's critique of the idea of "double consciousness," in *Race Matters* (Boston: Beacon Press, 1993), pp. 95-105.

18. Many economically depressed Hispanic communities reveal a deterioration of personal, familial, and communal relationships. When a people are deprived of these islands of human stability, it becomes almost impossible to develop within the people a critical consciousness, a moral commitment to or daring engagement for the cause of social transformation. In fact, public and communal life is almost completely disregarded, and only individual-personal accomplishment remains. The main problem confronted by successful individuals is how to use their resources and talents for things other than consumption and personal gratification.

19. Justo L. González, *Mañana: Christian Theology from a Hispanic Perspective* (Nashville: Abingdon Press, 1990), p. 40.

20. I reject the view of those who argue that if you do not speak "proper" Spanish you are not really Hispanic, just as I reject the view of those who argue that Spanish is culturally neutral when it comes to defining what being Hispanic is. We cannot penalize our brothers and sisters because their social context deprives them of the opportunity to learn and develop their language. Nor can we merely accept at face value the results of this unjust state of affairs, as if the loss of Spanish is an insignificant event for us. We must continue the political struggle to preserve bilingual education and a pluralistic cultural society. This is part of the struggle for the emancipation of our people and the affirmation of our identity.

21. Affirmative Action programs have fallen into great disrepute. This is one of the key achievements of the conservative forces that have dominated the political scene in the last twelve years. We must recall that there have always been Affirmative Action programs. Some were created as incentives to attract particular immigrants, others have supported farmers, others, soldiers. Most Hispanics recognize that these programs will not solve the extreme conditions of poverty experienced by our community. They will not overcome the extreme inequality that exists between the social classes at present in our society. But they are still important programs in that, without them, the economic and social condition of all communities will become worse than it already is. Racial prejudice and

attitudes of insensitivity toward racial and ethnic groups still influence the decision-making process of those who wield power. Compared with the security provided by the federal entitlement programs, the new drive to allow states to carry the burden of responsibility and to decide on public assistance programs creates an atmosphere of uncertainty among Hispanics and other racial and ethnic groups. It is also important to recall that the federal enforcement of the Voting Rights Act was a very significant factor in enhancing political participation and the gain of political offices by Latinos.

22. One of the dangers of this position is to emphasize ethnic pride by merely reacting against the racism that is prevalent in society. This negative and defensive posture is an inevitable element in the quest for self-identity. But one must also avoid falling into forms of Hispanic tribalism. We must recall that democratic politics works by numbers. If justice is our goal, we need to create coalitions with other racial and ethnic groups and other social groups that uphold principles and visions similar to ours, or that can provide support in solving problems we share in common, in spite of our moral and ideological differences.

23. This sentiment is being expressed in popular music even by conservative Hispanics. See, e.g., Gloria Estefan's song "Hablamos el mismo idioma" in her album *Mi Tierra.*

24. See the creative study done by F. M. Padilla, *Latino Ethnic Consciousness: The Case of Mexican Americans and Puerto Ricans in Chicago* (Notre Dame: University of Notre Dame Press, 1985). Also see M. Bernal and G. Knight, eds., *Ethnic Identity: Formation and Transmission Among Hispanics and Other Minorities* (Albany: State University of New York Press, 1993). David Maldonado also makes this point in his article "El Pueblo Latino and Its Identity: The Next Generation?" *Apuntes* 2 (1995): 45-57. James A. Regalos, in his article "Latino Representation in Los Angeles" (in Villarreal, Hernandez, and Neighbor, eds., *Latino Empowerment,* pp. 91-104), argues for the need to establish coalitions with other groups, in particular Asians and African Americans, as well as with liberal Jews and Anglo Saxons in order to consolidate power and increase political representation.

25. I am using the notion of the theological transfiguration of value developed by Warren R. Copeland, *Economic Justice: The Social Ethics of U.S. Economic Policy* (Nashville: Abingdon Press, 1988).

CHAPTER 3: THE THEOLOGICAL DIMENSION OF THE ETHICS OF CARE

1. God willing, Blessed be God, Be it as God wills, Holy Mary, God Bless you, Oh my God, God be with you.

2. Justo González has named this way of doing theology "Fuente Ovejuna," by which he means an enterprise that is done with la comunidad which provides the resources and lives the consequences of our reflections and options. This is the model that defines the process the Hispanic Instructors Group of Perkins School of Theology used in their theological reflection. Dr. Pedraja, Professor of Theology at Perkins School of Theology, defines this methodology as a "continual dialogue in which our voices join a chorus, without dissolving the tensions and differences we learn from each other's perspectives and create theology as a communal enterprise" (from critical responses to an earlier draft of *Dignidad*).

3. Francisco O. García Treto, "El Señor guarda a los emigrantes (Salmo 146:3)," *Apuntes* 4 (1981): 3-9. García Treto's treatment of God's care for the migrants is a good example of the way Hispanics are doing theology today. His work is the product of a community of interpretation which gathers the insights and views of Protestants, Catholic Hispanic and non-Hispanic exegetical scholars. It builds on the biblical notion of the God who cares for the poor. And his biblical work has a definite ethical and practical dimension which calls for the church to act faithfully. Finally, it uplifts principles and criteria relevant for public policy. Also see Jorge Lara-Braud, "Reflexiones teológicas sobre la migración," *Apuntes* 2 (1982): 3-7.

4. In Scripture, the elected, individuals or a people, are usually given difficult and demanding tasks that promise to improve the human condition. These tasks, mostly having to do with the enhancement of love and justice within the fabric of human relationships, are difficult and conflictual because they go against the dominion of the principalities and powers that rule the ways of the world. Those elected by God are given neither special protection nor advantages as they go about doing God's will. They are merely told to be intolerant and impatient with the suffering inflicted upon the innocent. However, they are also told that if they are made to suffer because of their faithfulness to God and their commitment to doing justice to the poor, they must endure and be patient with that suffering. In my view, this is at the heart of the Beatitudes.

5. For both a historical and a more-focused interpretation of the economical interpretation of the Trinity, see Justo L. González, *Mañana: Christian Theology from a Hispanic Perspective* (Nashville: Abingdon Press, 1990), pp. 101-15.

6. This is the theological basis for the transfiguration of values that I dealt with in chapter 2. This is one of the ways in which theology and our faith tradition enable us to redefine the values that inform our separate commitments and empower us to work in common.

7. González, *Mañana,* pp. 103-4.

8. The hierarchical mentality and the corresponding *caudillo* and *caciquismo* (charismatic, from the top centralized) style of political leadership, the passivity it instills in the people, and its relation to patriarchal dominance, are part of our legacy. It is vividly present in the process by which some native tribes conquered and subjugated other native tribes; and it consolidated itself with the conquest and colonization of the Americas. See Allan F. Deck, *The Second Wave: Hispanic Ministry and the Evangelization of Cultures* (Mahwah, N.J.: Paulist Press, 1989), p. 33.

9. No one expresses better the sense of dignity tied to one's body than people with AIDS. Many of these patients experience the indignity of seeing others create barriers between them and their bodies, when there is not danger of becoming infected. There is fear of touch, of a kiss, of a caress. And many who have come to terms with the fact that they will die soon, still agonize with the fear that their last remains will not be treated with dignity.

10. In a manner of speaking, we can say that sin has no independent reality. Sin is the distortion of the good. And the greater the good in question, the greater the possibility of its distortion and the greater the sin involved.

11. In our present culture we have come to believe that physicians play God, by which we mean not that they have the power to cure all, which we know they do not, but that they believe they owe no one account for what they do or attempt to do. In fairness, this is true of all professions and not just physicians. It is particularly true of professions that hold administrative and other "political" offices within any institution.

12. My colleague Dr. Pedraja, Professor of Theology at Perkins School of Theology, called my attention to the importance eschatology has for Hispanics. It is his claim that it is the awaited future of God's kingdom that allows Hispanics to see beyond their suffering to something better, which enables them to hope and remain committed against insurmountable odds in the struggle to improve their lives.

13. Christians have upheld many interpretations of the way love and justice are related to each other. Some argue that they are one and the same, and wonder why we have or need two terms. Others claim that they are different and conflicting terms, that is, that the demands of love violate those of justice. Others claim that love and justice are different but complementary. I am more inclined to see justice as a particular dimension of love, not the whole of love, but neither wholly different from it. For the best expression of this position see Jon Sobrino, *The True Church and the Poor* (Maryknoll, N.Y.: Orbis Books, 1984), pp. 39-63.

14. It is important to notice that though there are miracles that are left out of some of the gospel narratives, this story of Jesus reprimanding his disciples for pushing the women and children away appears in all four Gospels. This somewhat insignificant event ends up summarizing something at the heart of Jesus' message and purpose: that the socially devalued will be first in the Kingdom and that care and hospitality to the least of these affects and reveals one's sense of and commitment to the Kingdom.

15. These were some of the concerns Dr. Pedraja had with my emphasis on the image of the God who accompanies and suffers with us. In his view, to correct my emphasis one should be more explicit about the eschatological hope that is also at the heart of the Hispanic theological point of view. Hispanics, in his view, present to us the possibility of a triumphal God without the need to dominate and subjugate the other.

16. For a creative treatment of the topic of active patience in the epistle of James, see Eldin Villafañe, *Seek the Peace of the City: Reflections on Urban Ministry* (Grand Rapids, Mich.: Wm. B. Eerdmans Publishing Co., 1995); and Luis River Pagán, "La paciencia de la espera," *Apuntes* 2 (1981).

CHAPTER 4: THE CHURCH: A COMMUNITY OF RESISTANCE, A COMMUNITY FOR HUMAN DIGNITY

1. The term "church" is purposely left ambiguous. I am referring mostly to Protestant churches, and within the Protestant family to denominations described by the term "mainline." It is my contention, however, that, once the necessary revisions and nuances are taken into account, the claims I make are relevant to the Hispanic faith community at large.

2. The Nicene Creed (ecumenical).

3. Angela Erevia, "Particular Characteristics Towards a Pastoral Hispana," *Apuntes* 4 (1984): 11-13. The author stresses the dependence Hispanics feel on God and their providential sense of God's love. She also wants to encourage church leaders to work harder in assisting Hispanics to understand how the struggle for justice and the demand for recognition and respect for our human dignity are part of the church's pastoral care for its people.

4. In this chapter I am especially indebted to Justo L. González, *Out of Every Tribe and Nation: Christian Theology at the Ethnic Roundtable* (Nashville: Abingdon Press, 1992), pp. 100-114; Daniel L. Migliore, *Faith Seeking Understanding: An Introduction to Christian Ethics* (Grand Rapids, Mich.: Wm. B. Eerdmans Publishing Co., 1991), pp. 185-205; and Avery Dulles, *Models of the Church* (New York: Doubleday Image Books, 1974).

5. Two theological works that have helped me develop my theological perspective of human dignity are Jürgen Moltmann, *On Human Dignity: Political Theology and Ethics* (Philadelphia: Fortress Press, 1984), and Kathryn Tanner, *The Politics of God: Christian Theologies and Social Justice* (Minneapolis: Fortress Press, 1992).

6. I take it that the main purpose behind Harold Recinos' *Hear the Cry! Latino Pastor Challenges the Church* (Louisville: Westminster/John Knox Press, 1989) is precisely to show how it is possible for churches to move from a theological and pastoral perspective, which provides the poor with needed psychological comfort but with no concrete relief from the oppression they endure, to a theology and pastoral commitment that stresses the importance of social and institutional redemption for a genuine life of faith.

7. Justo makes it clear that what his roundtable discussion called the "quadrilateral of oppression" is a phenomenon that affects Hispanic churches as much as European American ones. "This quadrilateral of oppression includes *gender, class, culture,* and *race.* All four of these are employed as means of oppression, often playing one against the other. . . . It is quite common for ethnic minority churches to protest racial oppression, while in their midst women are kept out of decision-making positions. Likewise . . . white women . . . gather for a meal at church to discuss issues of women's liberation, while the meal itself is being prepared . . . by minority women whose wages leave much to be desired" (*Out of Every Tribe and Nation,* p. 104).

8. For a brief and interesting article that articulates some of the concerns with which we are dealing in this chapter from both Roman Catholic and Protestant points of view, see Bishop Elias Galvan, "Hispanics: Challenge and Opportunity," *Apuntes* 12 (1992): 89-97. Also see David Maldonado, "Hispanic Protestantism: Historical Reflections," *Apuntes* 11 (1991): 3-16. Maldonado claims that racism and ethnocentric cultural attitudes, rather than a desire to worship in Spanish, make "Mexican American families . . . drive past two or three Anglo Protestant Churches in order to reach the Hispanic Protestant Church across town. Hispanics and Anglos worship once a year in a 'fellowship' service, but become strangers the remainder of the year" (p. 14).

9. One of the main contributions many Hispanic evangelical and fundamentalist churches have offered to the Hispanic community is to provide rehabilitation centers and services for people, particularly the young, who are victims of drug addiction and of other types of substance abuse. Without in any way undermining their significant contribution in this area, it is still important to notice how they do not deal with the political dimension related to these issues that keeps this destructive principality and power within most poor Hispanic neighborhoods.

10. The work of Eldin Villafañe has been an attempt to articulate, on the basis of an evangelical theology and reading of Scripture, an argument for the necessity of social involvement in addition to a continuing commitment to personal spirituality. See his *Liberating Spirit: Towards an Hispanic American Pentecostal Social Ethic* (New York: University Press of America, 1992), and his article "An Evangelical Call to a Social Spirituality: Confronting Evil in Urban Society," *Apuntes* 11 (1991): 27-38. Harold Recinos argues that the apolitical, otherworldly, anti-Catholic, "blame-the-victim" attitudes and perceptions of many evangelical Hispanics are part and parcel of the missionary and colonial heritage. See his *Hear the Cry.* For a historical and more elaborate description of this oppressive mentality among Protestants, see Daniel R. Rodriguez-Diaz, "Los movimientos misioneros y el establecimiento de ideologias dominantes: 1800–1940," *Apuntes* 13 (1993).

11. This is true within both the Roman Catholic and the Protestant churches. The former has experiences of petrified institutionalization through the hierarchy, the latter through its polity and orthodoxy.

12. Yolanda E. Rivas, "Confrontación y reconciliación," *Apuntes* 2 (1982): 40-46. The author makes it clear that humility does not entail submissiveness to others. She also makes a strong case that we must be proud of who we are and confront our distorted images of ourselves as a first step toward being genuine servants of others. She is an advocate of group difference, not as an end in itself, but as a way toward the creation of solidarity groups that will enable us to transcend the fear, misery, prejudice, racism, and oppression that make it impossible for us to be reconciled to God and to one another.

13. During the 60s the Catholic Church organized the Partido Acción Cristiana to oppose the abortion laws and educational programs of the Partido Popular Democrático, the ruling political party of the time. The Church even threatened its faithful with excommunication if they voted for the P.P.D. The P.A.C. did extremely poorly in the polls, and the Church lost their moral authority for a significant amount of time.

14. Allan F. Deck, ed., *Frontiers of Hispanic Theology in the United States* (Maryknoll, N.Y.: Orbis Books, 1992). In his introduction to this anthology, Deck depicts quite well the relationship and differences between Latin American Theology of Liberation and the theology being created by Hispanics in the U.S.

15. In this section I am indebted to Stephen L. Carter, *The Culture of Disbelief: How American Law and Politics Trivialize Religious Devotion* (New York: Basic Books, 1993).

16. Jill Martinez, "In Search of an Inclusive Community," *Apuntes* 9 (1989): 3-9. Also see Michael G. Rival-Drunk, "The Challenge of Minority Identification and Enlistment of Ministry," *Apuntes* 5 (1985): 51-57. Both articles are written from a Protestant perspective; they both articulate some of the contributions and gifts Hispanics can bring to the church, and argue for the importance of ethnic pluralism if the church is to be truly catholic.

INDEX

INDEX

Printed in the United States
54063LVS00003B/195